GUITAR FOI

THE GUITAR METHOD FOR KIDS WHO WANNA ROCK!

BY BRIAN PARHAM
& SOPHIE PARHAM

ROCK DOJO THE COMPLETE BELT SYSTEM

 **PLAY ALONG**

ALL BACKING TRACKS AND AUDIO EXAMPLES ARE AVAILABLE AT:

WWW.ROCKDOJO.ORG/

PATENT PENDING

TABLE OF CONTENTS

"I WISH I COULD BE IN THE BAND,
BUT I DON'T WANT TO PRACTICE!"

WELCOME TO EIGHT QUARTERS OF ROCK GUITAR!

THE ROCK DOJO IS A GUITAR LEARNING METHOD BASED ON A SIMPLIFIED BELT SYSTEM.

TO EARN YOUR BELT:

1. LEARN YOUR BELT FOUNDATION AND PASS THE TEST
2. PERFORM TWO SONGS FROM THE FEATURED MUSICAL CONCEPT
3. COMPOSE YOUR OWN SONGS USING THE FEATURED MUSICAL CONCEPT

WHITE BELT ACHIEVEMENT

LEARN:

- KNOW YOUR GUITAR: PARTS OF THE GUITAR, HOW TO TUNE YOUR GUITAR, NAMES OF THE OPEN STRINGS
- PLAYING IN THE POCKET: BASIC RHYTHMS
- THE MUSICAL ALPHABET

PLAY:

- ☆ GUITAR PART FOR 2 SONGS

COMPOSE:

- YOUR OWN SONG USING THE FEATURED MUSICAL CONCEPT

GREEN BELT ACHIEVEMENT

LEARN:

- OPEN CHORDS
- AMP SETTINGS: DIAL IN THE PERFECT TONE
- SYNCOPATED RHYTHMS

PLAY:

- ☆ GUITAR PART FOR 2 SONGS

COMPOSE:

- YOUR OWN SONG USING THE FEATURED MUSICAL CONCEPT AND BASIC SONG FORM

YELLOW BELT ACHIEVEMENT

LEARN:

- THE NAMES OF THE NOTES ON THE E & A STRINGS & MOVEABLE POWER CHORDS
- GUITAR TABLATURE
- ROCK BAND: THE ROLES OF EACH INSTRUMENT

PLAY:

- ☆ GUITAR PART FOR 2 SONGS

COMPOSE:

- YOUR OWN SONG USING THE FEATURED MUSICAL CONCEPT

RED BELT ACHIEVEMENT

LEARN:

- ROCK SOLOING 101: THE PENTATONICS
- THREE EASY LICKS
- BASIC SONG FORM

PLAY:

- ☆☆☆ GUITAR PARTS FOR 2 SONGS
- SOLO OVER SONSG

COMPOSE:

- YOUR OWN SONG USING THE FEATURED MUSICAL CONCEPT

BLACK BELT ACHIEVEMENT

LEARN:

- ROCK SOLOING 102: REPEATING LICKS
- 16TH NOTES
- HISTORY OF ROCK GUITAR

PLAY:

- ★ ★ ★ GUITAR PARTS FOR 2 SONGS
- SOLO OVER SONGS

COMPOSE:

- CHOOSE TWO MUSICAL CONCEPTS AND COMPOSE A SONG WITH AN A & B SECTION

AND:

HELP OTHER STUDENTS ALONG THEIR MUSICAL JOURNEYS!

SET YOUR GOALS

NAME: _____ **DATE:** _____ **GRADE:** _____

EARN WHITE BELT

I WILL PRACTICE _____ MINUTES PER DAY, _____ DAYS PER WEEK.

DATE ACHIEVED: _____

START DATE: _____

WHEN IT GETS HARD, I WILL: _____

I CAN DO IT BECAUSE: _____

MY REWARD: _____

EARN YELLOW BELT

I WILL PRACTICE _____ MINUTES PER DAY, _____ DAYS PER WEEK.

DATE ACHIEVED: _____

START DATE: _____

WHEN IT GETS HARD, I WILL: _____

I CAN DO IT BECAUSE: _____

MY REWARD: _____

EARN GREEN BELT

I WILL PRACTICE _____ MINUTES PER DAY, _____ DAYS PER WEEK.

DATE ACHIEVED: _____

START DATE: _____

WHEN IT GETS HARD, I WILL: _____

I CAN DO IT BECAUSE: _____

MY REWARD: _____

EARN RED BELT

I WILL PRACTICE _____ MINUTES PER DAY, _____ DAYS PER WEEK.

DATE ACHIEVED: _____

START DATE: _____

WHEN IT GETS HARD, I WILL: _____

I CAN DO IT BECAUSE: _____

MY REWARD: _____

EARN BLACK BELT

I WILL PRACTICE [____] MINUTES PER DAY, [____] DAYS PER WEEK.

DATE ACHIEVED: [____]

START DATE: _____

WHEN IT GETS HARD, I WILL: _____

I CAN DO IT BECAUSE: _____

MY REWARD: _____

REMEMBER

The Virtuous Circle of Practice

The More You Practice ...

The Better You Get ...

The Better You Get ...

ROCK DOJO — Guitar Lessons for Kids — *Who Wanna Rock!*

BELTS	STRIPES	SEPTEMBER	OCTOBER	NOVEMBER	DECEMBER	JANUARY	FEBRUARY	MARCH	APRIL	MAY	JUNE	JULY	AUGUST	SEPTEMBER	OCTOBER	NOVEMBER	DECEMBER	JANUARY	FEBRUARY	MARCH	APRIL	MAY	JUNE	JULY	AUGUST	SEPTEMBER

GUITAR SIZING CHART FOR KIDS

¼ SIZE	½ SIZE	¾ SIZE	FULL SIZE
4 TO 6 YEARS OLD	5 TO 8 YEARS OLD	8 TO 11 YEARS OLD	11+ YEARS OLD
3'3" TO 3'9"	3'10" TO 4'5"	4'6" TO 4'11"	5' AND OVER

WWW.ROCKDOJO.ORG
(503) 484-6417

ZOMBIE BOY'S TOP 10 TIPS FOR GUITAR ~~GREATNESS:~~

1	NEVER TUNE YOUR GUITAR. IT'S BORING.
2	NEVER TAKE THE TIME TO LEARN TO TUNE YOUR GUITAR. WHY? SEE POINT #1.
3	NEVER PRACTICE. IT'S USELESS.
4	AT THE END OF THE WEEK, SAY YOU PRACTICED EVEN THOUGH YOU DIDN'T. YOUR TEACHER WILL NEVER KNOW THE DIFFERENCE.
5	MAKE EXCUSES FOR NOT PRACTICING. "I DIDN'T PRACTICE BECAUSE A WEREWOLF ATE MY GUITAR." YOUR TEACHER WILL BE TOTALLY FOOLED.
6	NEVER—UNDER ANY CIRCUMSTANCE— COUNT OUT RHYTHMS. IT'S A TOTAL WASTE OF TIME!
7	ALWAYS PRACTICE AS FAST AS POSSIBLE. AFTER ALL, YOU CAN MASTER EVERY LICK THE FIRST TIME YOU ENCOUNTER IT.
8	NEVER LISTEN TO ANY MUSIC.
9	WHEN PLAYING IN AN ENSEMBLE, ALWAYS RUSH AHEAD OF THE TEMPO. EVERYONE WILL BE BLOWN AWAY!
10	IGNORE YOUR AMP SETTINGS. JUST CRANK THE VOLUME AND OVERDRIVE UP TO 10!
BONUS TIP!!!	WHEN YOUR TEACHER EXPLAINS A MUSICAL CONCEPT TO THE CLASS, THIS IS YOUR MOMENT TO SHINE! NOODLE AS FAST AND AS LOUD AS YOU CAN.

WWW.ROCKDOJO.ORG
(503) 484-6417

FIVE REAL PRACTICE TIPS FOR MASTERING THE GUITAR

I. LESS IS MORE: FOCUS ON ONE OR TWO TECHNIQUES, CONCEPTS, OR SONGS AT A TIME. IDEALLY, YOU SHOULD PRACTICE EVERY DAY FOR AT LEAST 10-15 MINUTES.

II. SLOWER IS BETTER: BELIEVE IT OR NOT, SLOWER IS FASTER WHEN IT COMES TO THE GUITAR, SO IF YOU WANT TO PLAY FAST, PRACTICE SLOWLY. REALLY, REALLY S-L-O-W WITH PERFECT RHYTHM. OVER TIME, GRADUALLY INCREASE THE TEMPO.

III. PLAY IT LIKE YOU MEAN IT: PLAY EVERY MEASURE EXACTLY THE WAY YOU HEAR IT IN YOUR HEAD.

IV. ALWAYS PRACTICE WITH A BEAT: PRACTICING FOR 15-MINUTES WITH A METRONOME OR A BACKING TRACK IS WORTH MORE THAN AN HOUR OF PRACTICE WITHOUT. LIVE BY THIS RULE, SWEAR BY IT, AND YOU'LL SEPARATE YOURSELF FROM 95% OF THE OTHER KIDS TRYING TO LEARN TO PLAY GUITAR.

V. LEARN FROM THE MASTERS: LISTEN TO SOME MUSIC EVERYDAY. IF YOU DON'T KNOW WHERE TO START, LOOK THROUGH THIS BOOK FOR INSPIRATION. ONCE YOU FIND AN ARTIST OR A BAND YOU LIKE, TRY A FULL ALBUM. LISTENING TO MUSIC EVERY DAY WILL CULTIVATE YOUR EARS, BROADEN YOUR MUSICAL HORIZONS, AND HELP YOU DEVELOP YOUR OWN SIGNATURE SOUND!

FINGER WORKOUT: WARM UP BEFORE SHREDDING!

LIKE LOTS OF FUN THINGS IN LIFE SUCH AS KARATE, SOCCER, OR SINGING, PLAYING ROCK GUITAR REQUIRES A WARM UP.

Q: ONE SCHOOL QUARTER EQUALS 10 WEEKS
ASCENDING: FROM LOW E (BIG E) TO HIGH E (LITTLE E)
DESCENDING: FROM HIGH E (LITTLE E) TO LOW E (BIG E)
REMEMBER: ALWAYS USE ONE FINGER PER FRET!

Q1: ASCENDING 1,2,3,4 DESCENDING 4,3,2,1

Q2: ASCENDING 2,3,4,1 DESCENDING 3,2,1,4

Q3: ASCENDING 1,4,3,2 DESCENDING 4,1,2,3

Q4: ASCENDING 2,1,4,3 DESCENDING 3,4,1,2

Q5: ASCENDING 1,2,4,3 DESCENDING 4,3,1,2

Q6: ASCENDING 2,1,3,4 DESCENDING 3,4,2,1

Q7: ASCENDING 1,3,4,2 DESCENDING 4,1,3,2

Q8: ASCENDING 2,3,1,4 DESCENDING 3,2,4,1

THIS IS YOUR FRETTING HAND

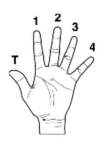

WHITE BELT

FOUNDATIONS

KNOW YOUR GUITAR

ELECTRIC GUITAR

THE ELECTRIC GUITAR IS THE HEART AND SOUL OF ROCK MUSIC. IN THE HANDS OF A MASTER GUITARISTS, THE ELECTRIC GUITAR CAN CRY AND SQUEAL AND SCREAM, OR IT CAN SOUND AS SOFT AND AS TENDER AS A NEWBORN KITTEN.

ELECTRIC GUITARS ARE TYPICALLY THINNER AND EASIER FOR BEGINNERS TO HOLD. BUT REMEMBER THIS: ELECTRIC GUITARS REQUIRE AMPLIFIERS.

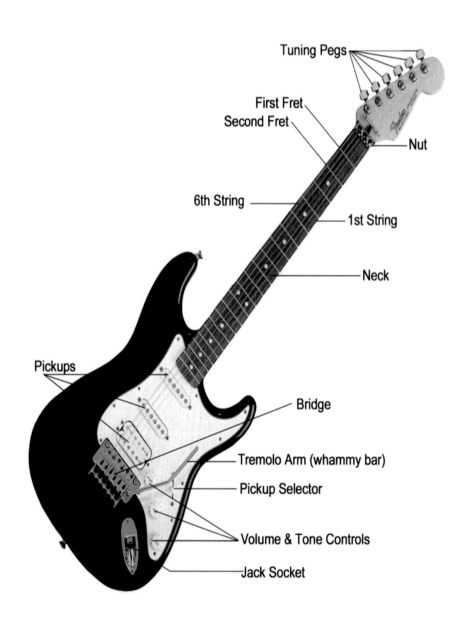

Tuning Pegs
First Fret
Second Fret
Nut
6th String
1st String
Neck
Pickups
Bridge
Tremolo Arm (whammy bar)
Pickup Selector
Volume & Tone Controls
Jack Socket

ACOUSTIC GUITAR

THE ACOUSTIC GUITAR HAS A RICH, FULL-BODY SOUND GREAT FOR CREATING RHYTHM GUITAR PARTS OR FOR ACCOMPANYING SINGERS. THEY COME IN THREE DIFFERENT SIZES: FULL SIZE, ¾ SIZE, AND ½ SIZE. WHEN CHOOSING A GUITAR, CHOOSE THE INSTRUMENT THAT BEST FITS YOU.

GUITARS ALSO COME IN NYLON OR STEEL-STRING VARIETIES. ALTHOUGH THE STEEL-STRING ACOUSTIC GUITAR IS GENERALLY THE PREFERRED ACOUSTIC INSTRUMENT FOR ROCK MUSIC, SMALL CHILDREN OFTEN FIND STEEL STRINGS DIFFICULT TO FRET AND PAINFUL FOR THE TIPS OF THEIR FINGERS.

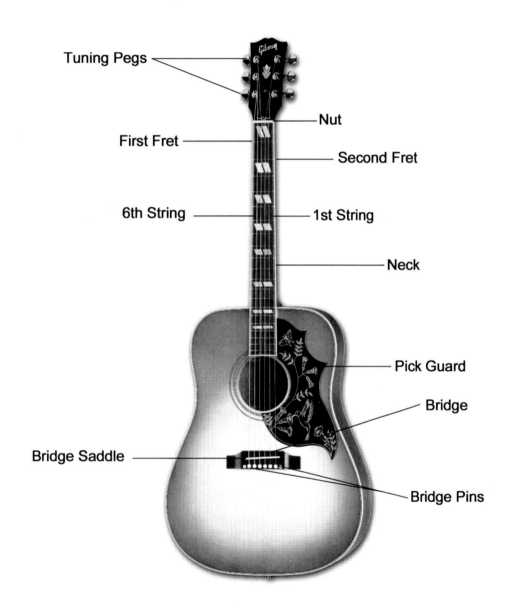

TUNE YOUR GUITAR

NAME OF THE GUITAR STRINGS

"Eddie Ate Dynamite Good Bye Eddie"

E A D G B E

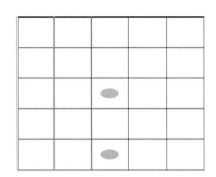

ALWAYS TUNE YOUR GUITAR BEFORE YOU PLAY IT! THE EASIEST WAY TO TUNE THE GUITAR IS TO USE AN ELECTRONIC TUNER. THEY'RE CHEAP, EASY-TO-USE, AND READILY AVAILABLE.

ELECTRONIC TUNERS:

PLAYING IN THE POCKET: BASIC RHYTHMS

BEATS	NOTE VALUE	RESTS
4	𝆶	▬
2	𝅗𝅥	▬
1	♩	𝄽
0.5	♪	𝄾
0.25	♬	𝄿

THE POCKET IS THE RHYTHMIC GLUE THAT BINDS A BAND OR A SONG TOGETHER. PLAYING IN THE POCKET HAPPENS WHEN A MUSICIAN FINDS HIS/HER SPACE IN THE MUSIC WHILE SIMULTANEOUSLY LEAVING SPACE FOR THE OTHER BANDMATES TO OCCUPY. WHEN A BAND PLAYS IN THE POCKET, SOMETHING MAGICAL HAPPENS: THE MUSIC FEELS GOOD, THE GROOVE TAKES OVER, AND THE LISTENING AUDIENCE BECOMES COMPELLED TO DANCE.

THE MUSICAL ALPHABET

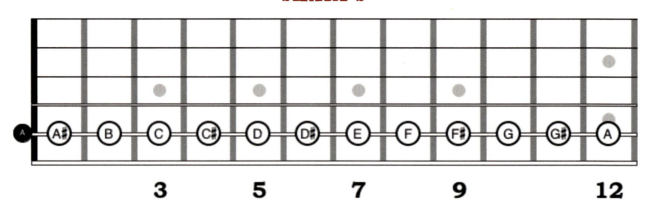

SHARPS

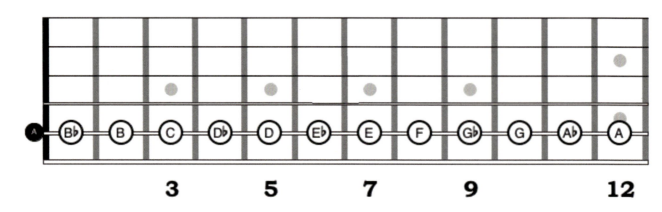

FLATS

"THERE ARE NO SHARPS OR FLATS BETWEEN **B** AND **C**, AND THERE ARE NO SHARPS OR FLATS STEP BETWEEN **E** AND **F**!"

MNEMONIC DEVICE:

"**B**ERNIE **C**OHEN AND **E**RNIE **F**RANK ARE TWO CLOSE FRIENDS OF MINE."

WHITE BELT FOUNDATIONS TEST

I. PARTS OF THE GUITAR

COMPLETE THE FOLLOWING DIAGRAM:

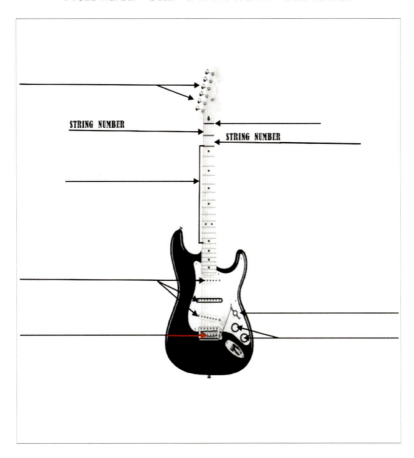

II. TUNE YOUR GUITAR

E A D G B E

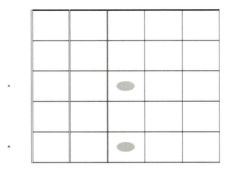

"Eddie Ate Dynamite Good Bye Eddie"

III. PLAYING IN THE POCKET: BASIC RHYTHMS

CLAP THE FOLLOWING RHYTHM:

$$\| \, \circ \, | \, \downarrow \; \downarrow \; \downarrow \; \downarrow \, | \, \downarrow \; \downarrow \, | \, \circ \, \|$$

IV. THE MUSICAL ALPHABET

COMPLETE THE FOLLOWING SENTENCES:

"THERE ARE NO SHARPS OR FLATS BETWEEN ___ AND ___, AND THERE ARE NO SHARPS OR FLATS STEP BETWEEN ___ AND ___!"

"_____ _____ AND _____ _____ ARE TWO CLOSE FRIENDS OF MINE."

SHARPS

→ A A♯ B __ C♯ D __ E __ __ __ G♯

FLATS

__ B♭ __ C D♭ __ E♭ __ F __ G A♭ ←

ROCK ON!

YELLOW BELT

FOUNDATIONS

NOTES ON THE 6TH AND 5TH STRINGS

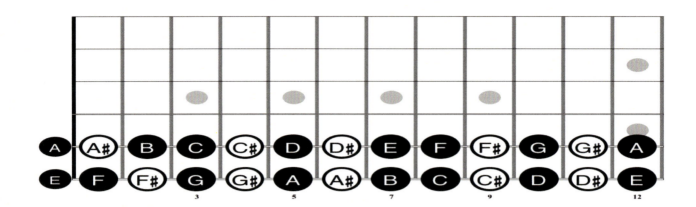

MOVEABLE POWER CHORDS

POWER CHORDS ARE TWO NOTE CHORDS (ROOT AND 5TH) NAMED AFTER THE ROOT NOTE YOU PLAY ON THE 6TH OR 5TH STRING WITH YOUR INDEX FINGER.

6TH STRING ROOT POWER CHORD (G5):

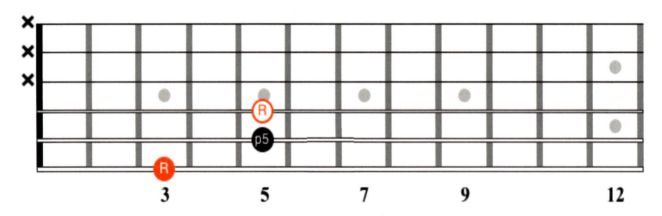

5TH STRING ROOT POWER CHORD (C5):

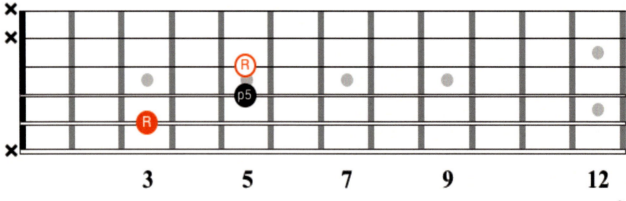

THE ROCK BAND

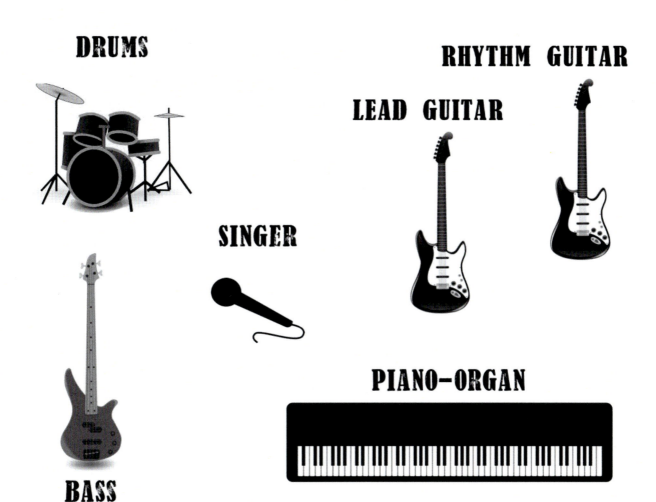

DRUMS

RHYTHM GUITAR

LEAD GUITAR

SINGER

PIANO-ORGAN

BASS

DRUMS: THE DRUMMER ESTABLISHES THE BEAT OF THE SONG. THE DRUMS ARE THE BACKBONE OF THE BAND AND KEEP THE SONG TOGETHER.

BASS GUITAR: THE BASSIST TYPICALLY HIGHLIGHTS THE CHORDS ROOTS AND PROVIDES RHYTHMIC AND HARMONIC FOUNDATION FOR THE BAND.

THE KEYS (PIANO/HAMMOND ORGAN/SYNTHETIZER): THE KEYBOARDIST PLAYS A SUPPORTIVE ROLE IN MOST ROCK BANDS. THE KEYS ADD DEPTH TO THE MUSIC BY PLAYING CHORDS & MELODIC FILLS, PROVIDING TEXTURES, OR EVEN IMITATING OTHER INSTRUMENTS THROUGH THE USE OF SOUND PATCHES.

RHYTHM GUITAR: THE RHYTHM GUITARIST PLAYS CHORDS AND PROVIDES RHYTHMIC SUPPORT FOR THE BAND.

LEAD GUITAR: THE LEAD GUITARIST PLAYS SINGLE NOTE MELODY LINES OR DOUBLE STOPS.

SINGER: THE LEAD VOCALIST SINGS THE MELODY AND LEADS ALL SINGING IN THE GROUP.

REMEMBER: NO RHYTHM/NO MUSIC

GUITAR TABLATURE

READING GUITAR TABLATURE IS EASY. THE SIX LINES REPRESENT THE SIX STRINGS OF THE GUITAR. IN FACT, IT'S LIKE LOOKING AT YOUR GUITAR UPSIDE DOWN. THE BOTTOM LINE REPRESENTS THE LOWEST, THICKEST STRING WHILE THE TOP LINE REPRESENTS THE HIGHEST, THINNEST STRING. THE NUMBERS REPRESENT THE FRETTED NOTE.

DOES IT GET ANY EASIER THAN THAT?

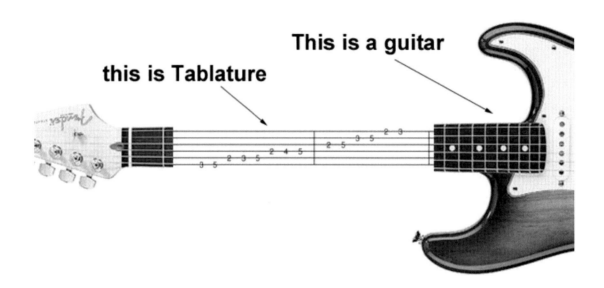

IN OTHER WORDS,

Write your own music using Tablature

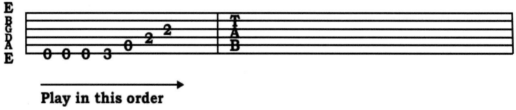

Play in this order

Fret Numbers: 0 3 2

YELLOW BELT FOUNDATIONS TEST

I. NOTES ON THE 6TH & 5TH STRINGS

LABEL THE NOTE NAMES ON THE 6TH STRING:

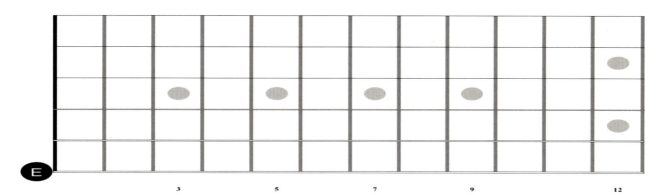

LABEL THE NOTE NAMES ON THE 5TH STRING:

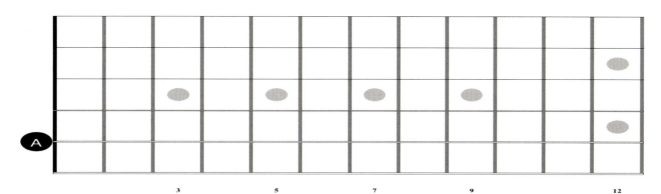

II. MOVEABLE POWER CHORDS

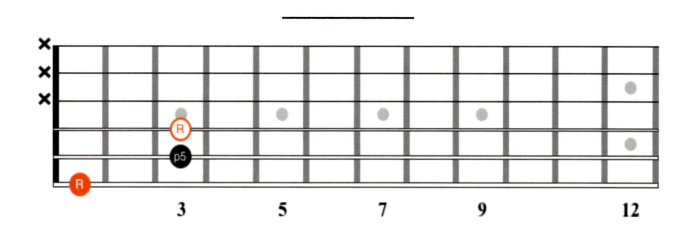

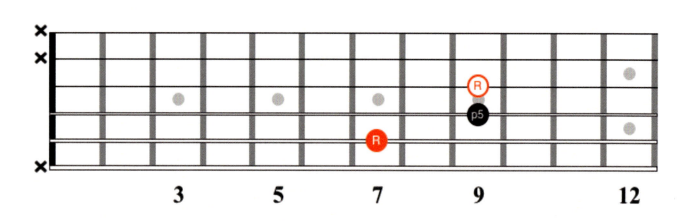

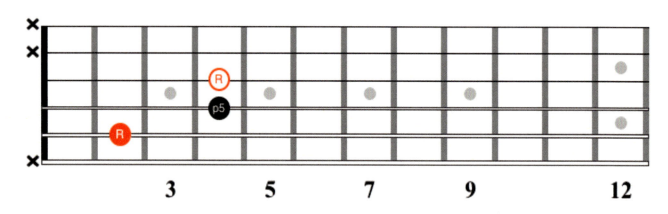

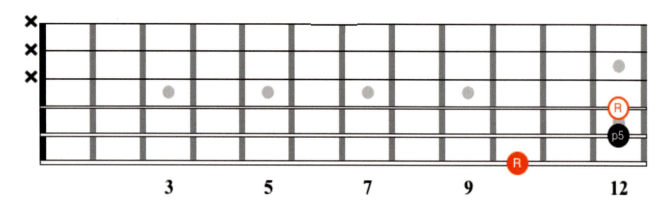

III. THE ROCK BAND

MATCH THE CORRECT INSTRUMENT WITH IT'S ROLE IN THE BAND:

A. BASS GUITAR	_____. PLAYS SINGLE NOTE MELODY LINES OR DOUBLE STOPS.
B. RHYTHM GUITAR	_____. ESTABLISH THE BEAT OF THE SONG. THIS INSTRUMENT IS THE BACKBONE OF THE BAND AND KEEPS THE SONG TOGETHER.
C. SINGER	_____. SINGS THE MELODY AND LEADS ALL SINGING IN THE GROUP.
D. LEAD GUITAR	_____. PLAYS CHORDS AND PROVIDES RHYTHMIC SUPPORT FOR THE BAND.
E. THE KEYS	_____. TYPICALLY HIGHLIGHTS THE CHORDS ROOTS AND PROVIDES RHYTHMIC AND HARMONIC FOUNDATION FOR THE BAND.
F. DRUMS	_____. PLAYS A SUPPORTIVE ROLE IN MOST ROCK BANDS. THIS INSTRUMENT ADDS DEPTH TO THE MUSIC BY PLAYING CHORDS & MELODIC FILLS, PROVIDING TEXTURES, OR EVEN IMITATING OTHER INSTRUMENTS THROUGH THE USE OF SOUND PATCHES.

IV. GUITAR TABLATURE

TAB THE FOLLOWING POWER CHORDS:

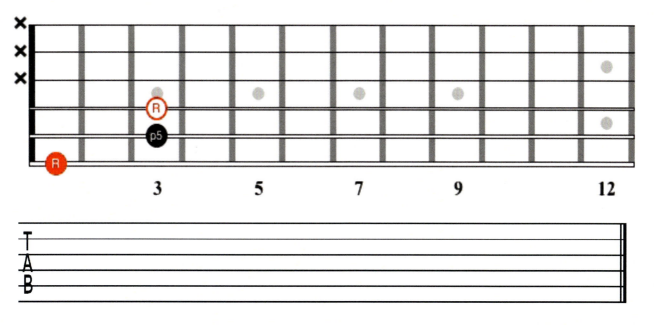

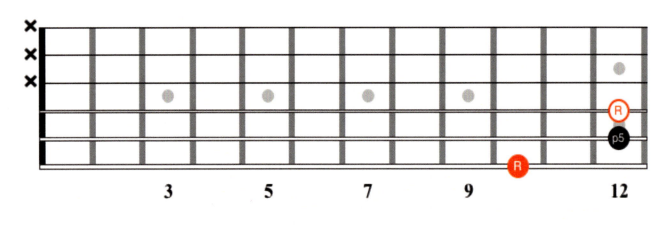

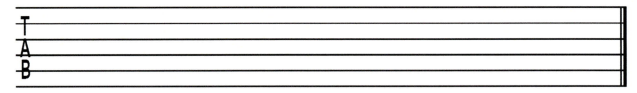

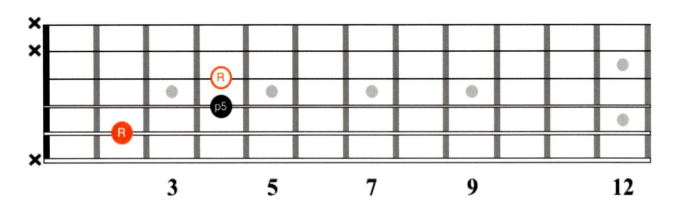

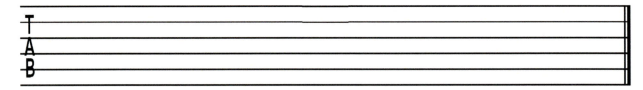

ROCK ON!

GREEN BELT

FOUNDATIONS

OPEN CHORDS

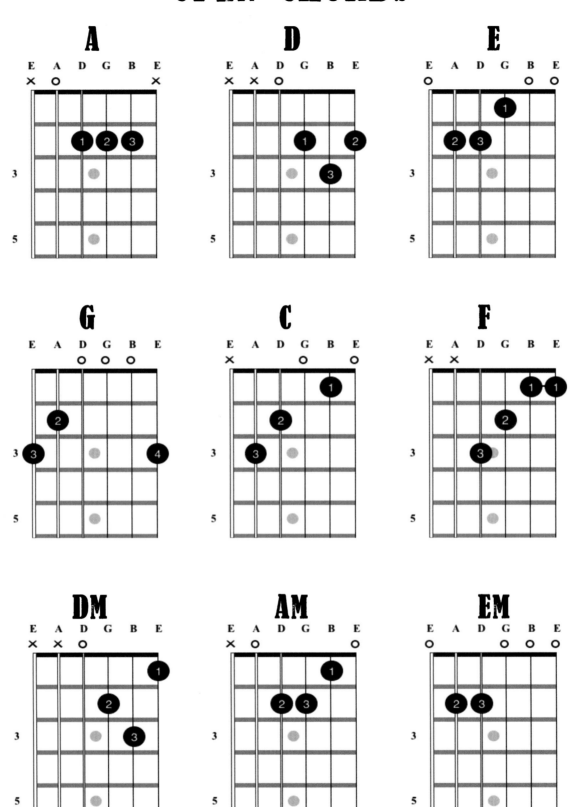

KNOW YOUR GUITAR AMPLIFIER

BETTER KNOWN AS "THE AMP"

AN ELECTRIC GUITAR WITHOUT AN AMP IS LIKE THE SOUND OF ONE HAND CLAPPING. IN OTHER WORDS, THE AMP GIVES SOUND, POWER, AND SONIC POSSIBILITIES TO YOUR ELECTRIC GUITAR. WITHOUT YOUR AMP, THE ELECTRIC GUITAR IS MUTE.

NOW, LET'S REVIEW SOME IMPORTANT FUNCTIONS OF THE AMPLIFIER.

GAIN: CONTROLS POWER OF ELECTRIC SIGNAL. MORE POWER = MORE OVERDRIVE.

VOLUME: CONTROLS LOUDNESS.

TREBLE: CONTROLS THE HIGH-END FREQUENCIES ADDING BRIGHTNESS & SHIMMER TO THE SOUND.

BASS: CONTROLS THE LOW-END FREQUENCIES ADDING DEPTH & ROUNDNESS TO THE SOUND.

MASTER: CONTROLS THE OVERALL VOLUME OF THE AMPLIFIER.

DELAY/REVERB/ECHO: REPLICATES THE EFFECT OF A GUITAR PLAYING IN A CAVE, A CANYON, OR A CATHEDRAL.

DON'T FORGET ABOUT THE VOLUME & TONE KNOBS ON YOUR GUITAR!

SYNCOPATED RHYTHMS

SYNCOPATION: IS THE EMPHASIS OF WEAK BEATS.

STRONG BEATS: 1 + 2 + 3 + 4 +

WEAK BEATS: 1 + 2 + 3 + 4 +

SYNCOPATED	NOT-SYNCOPATED
1 **+** 2 **+** 3 **+** 4 **+**	**1** + **2** + **3** + **4** +
| ♪ ♪ ♪ ♪ ♪ ♪ ♪ ♪ |	| ♩ ♩ ♩ ♩ |
1 + 2 **+** 3 + 4 +	**1** + **2** + **3** + 4 +
| ♩. ♪ ♩ |	| ♩ ♩ ♩ |
1 + **2** **+** 3 **+** 4 +	**1** + **2** **+** 3 + 4 +
| ♩ ♩ ♫ ♪ 𝄾 |	| ♩ ♩ ♫ ♩ 𝄾 |

SYNCOPATED RHYTHMS ADD EXCITEMENT AND PLAYFULNESS TO MUSIC. WITHOUT SYNCOPATED RHYTHMS, MUSIC WOULD SOUND STIFF AND ROBOTIC.

GREEN BELT FOUNDATIONS TEST

I. OPEN CHORDS

CORRECTLY NAME THE FOLLOWING CHORDS:

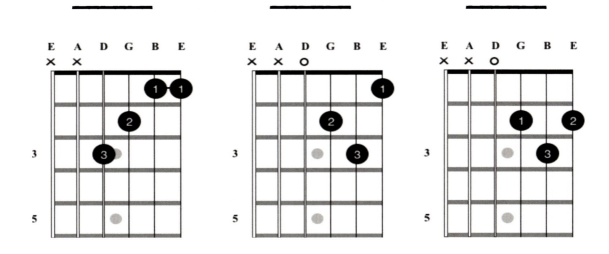

PLAY THROUGH THE FOLLOWING CHORD PROGRESSIONS:

‖ G | D | EM | C ‖

&

‖ AM | C | G | F ‖

II. KNOW YOUR AMP

MATCH THE CORRECT INSTRUMENT WITH IT'S ROLE IN THE BAND:

A. TREBLE	_____. REPLICATES THE EFFECT OF YOUR GUITAR PLAYING IN A CAVE, A CANYON, OR A CATHEDRAL.
B. DELAY/REVERB/ECHO	_____. CONTROLS LOUDNESS.
C. VOLUME	_____. CONTROLS THE HIGH-END FREQUENCIES ADDING BRIGHTNESS & SHIMMER TO THE SOUND.
D. GAIN	_____. CONTROLS POWER OF ELECTRIC SIGNAL. MORE POWER = MORE OVERDRIVE.
E. MASTER	_____. CONTROLS THE LOW-END FREQUENCIES ADDING DEPTH AND ROUNDNESS TO THE SOUND.
F. BASS	_____. CONTROLS THE OVERALL VOLUME OF THE AMPLIFIER.

III. SYNCOPATED RHYTHMS

CLAP THE FOLLOWING RHYTHMS:

1. | 𝅘𝅥. 𝅘𝅥𝅮 𝅗𝅥 |

2. | 𝅘𝅥. 𝅘𝅥𝅮 𝅘𝅥𝅮𝅘𝅥𝅮 𝅘𝅥 |

3.

4. | 𝄾 ♪ ♩ ♫♫ |

5. | ♩ ♫ ♫ 𝄾 ♪ |

6. | ♩ 𝄾 ♪ 𝄾 ♪ |

ROCK ON!

RED BELT

FOUNDATIONS

ROCK SOLOING 101: THE MINOR PENTATONIC SCALE

MINOR PENTATONIC SCALE	=	1 b3 4 5 b7
A MINOR PENTATONIC SCALE	=	A C D E G

THE A MINOR PENTATONIC SCALE:

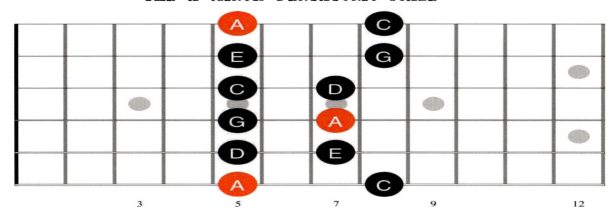

THE MINOR PENTATONIC SCALE IS USED TO SOLO OVER MINOR CHORD PROGRESSIONS. FOR EXAMPLE, USE THE A MINOR PENTATONIC SCALE TO SOLO OVER THE FOLLOWING CHORD PROGRESSION:

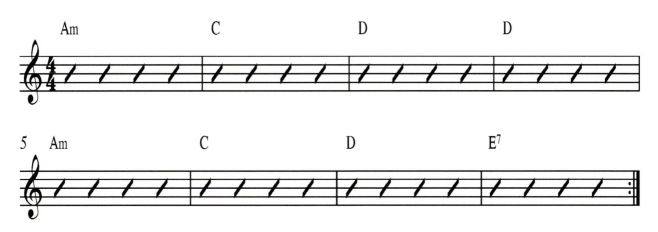

ROCK SOLOING 102: THE MAJOR PENTATONIC SCALE

THE MAJOR PENTATONIC SCALE	=	1 2 3 5 6
A MAJOR PENTATONIC SCALE	=	A B C# E F#

A MAJOR PENTATONIC SCALE:

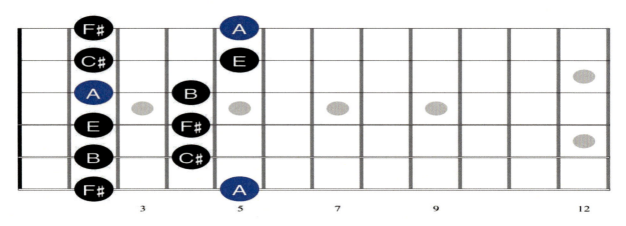

THE MAJOR PENTATONIC SCALE IS USED TO SOLO OVER MAJOR CHORD PROGRESSIONS. FOR EXAMPLE, USE THE A MAJOR PENTATONIC SCALE TO SOLO OVER THE FOLLOWING CHORD PROGRESSION:

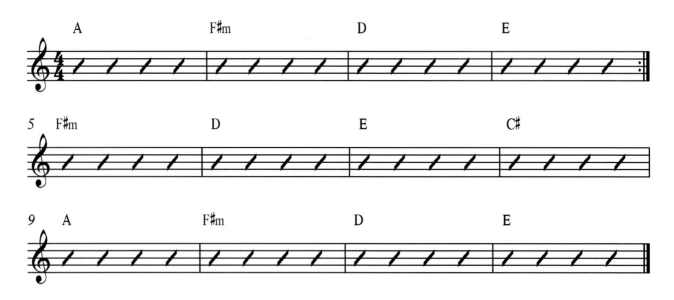

THREE EASY LICKS

A LICK IS A SHORT MUSICAL STATEMENT. JUST LIKE WORDS IN SPOKEN LANGUAGE, MUSICIANS COMBINE LICKS TO TELL STORIES.

37

BASIC SONG FORM

THERE ARE MANY DIFFERENT SONG FORMS, BUT THE ABABCB SONG STRUCTURE IS ONE OF THE MOST COMMON SONG FORMS IN ROCK & POP MUSIC.

ABABCB
INTRO
VERSE 1
CHORUS 1
VERSE 2
CHORUS 2
BRIDGE + SOLO
CHORUS 3
OUTRO

INTRO: SETS THE MOOD OF THE SONG.

VERSE: LEADS TO THE CHORUS.

CHORUS: THE BIG STATEMENT.

SOLO: FEATURES ONE OF THE MUSICIANS IN PARTICULAR, SUCH AS THE KEYBOARDS, SAXOPHONIST, OR THE GUITARIST.

BRIDGE: LINKS TWO SECTIONS OF A SONG TOGETHER JUST LIKE AN ACTUAL BRIDGE.

OUTRO: ENDS THE SONG.

RED BELT FOUNDATIONS TEST

I. ROCK SOLOING: THE PENTATONIC SCALES

WHICH SCALE WOULD YOU USE TO SOLO OVER THE FOLLOWING CHORD PROGRESSIONS?

‖ C | AM | F | G ‖

&

‖ CM | Eb | FM | FM ‖

II. II. THREE EASY LICKS:

PLAY ALL THREE LICKS OVER THE FOLLOWING CHORD PROGRESSION:

‖ CM | Eb | FM | FM ‖

III. BASIC SONG FORM

ARRANGE THE FOLLOWING SECTIONS INTO THE WORLD'S MOST COMMON SONG-STRUCTURE:

ABABCB

BRIDGE + SOLO	_____
CHORUS 3	_____
CHORUS 1	_____
BRIDGE + SOLO	_____
INTRO	_____
CHORUS 2	_____
VERSE 2	_____
VERSE 1	_____

CIRCLE THE CORRECT DEFINITION FOR EACH SONG SECTION:

THE CHORUS IS:

A. ENDS THE SONG.

B. THE BIG STATEMENT.

C. LINKS TWO SECTIONS OF THE SONG TOGETHER.

THE BRIDGE IS USED TO:

A. LINK TWO SECTIONS OF THE SONG TOGETHER.

B. LEAD TO THE CHORUS.

C. FEATURE ONE OF THE MUSICIANS IN PARTICULAR, SUCH AS THE KEYBOARDS, SAXOPHONIST, OR THE GUITARIST.

THE VERSE:

A. SETS THE MOOD OF THE SONG.

B. ENDS THE SONG.

C. LEADS TO THE CHORUS.

BLACK BELT

FOUNDATIONS

16TH NOTES

BEATS CAN BE EVENLY DIVIDED LIKE THIS:

𝅝	=	𝅗𝅥 𝅗𝅥
𝅗𝅥	=	𝅘𝅥 𝅘𝅥
𝅘𝅥	=	𝅘𝅥𝅮 𝅘𝅥𝅮
𝅘𝅥𝅮	=	𝅘𝅥𝅯 𝅘𝅥𝅯 𝅘𝅥𝅯 𝅘𝅥𝅯

A SIXTEENTH NOTE IS ONE/SIXTEENTH THE VALUE OF A WHOLE NOTE.

𝅝 = 𝅘𝅥𝅯𝅘𝅥𝅯𝅘𝅥𝅯𝅘𝅥𝅯 𝅘𝅥𝅯𝅘𝅥𝅯𝅘𝅥𝅯𝅘𝅥𝅯 𝅘𝅥𝅯𝅘𝅥𝅯𝅘𝅥𝅯𝅘𝅥𝅯 𝅘𝅥𝅯𝅘𝅥𝅯𝅘𝅥𝅯𝅘𝅥𝅯

IN OTHER WORDS:

𝅗𝅥 = 𝅘𝅥𝅯𝅘𝅥𝅯𝅘𝅥𝅯𝅘𝅥𝅯 𝅘𝅥𝅯𝅘𝅥𝅯𝅘𝅥𝅯𝅘𝅥𝅯

AND:

𝅘𝅥 = 𝅘𝅥𝅯𝅘𝅥𝅯𝅘𝅥𝅯𝅘𝅥𝅯

AND FINALLY:

𝅘𝅥𝅮 = 𝅘𝅥𝅯𝅘𝅥𝅯

COUNTING 16ᵀᴴ NOTES

1   E   +   A
OR
TI-KI-TI-KI

EXAMPLE 1:

1   2   3   E   +   A   4
OR
TA   TA   TI-KI-TI-KI   TA

EXAMPLE 2:

1   2   +   3   +   4   E   +   A
OR
TA   TI-TI   TI-TI   TI-KI-TI-KI

EXAMPLE 3:

1   E   +   A   2   3   E   +   A   4
OR
TI-KI-TI-KI   SH   TI-KI-TI-KI   SH

ROCK SOLOING 201: REPEATING LICKS

REPEATING LICKS ADD TENSION AND EXCITEMENT TO GUITAR SOLOS.

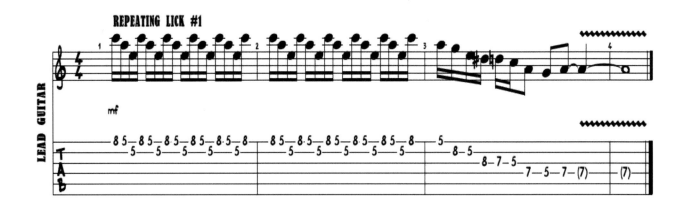

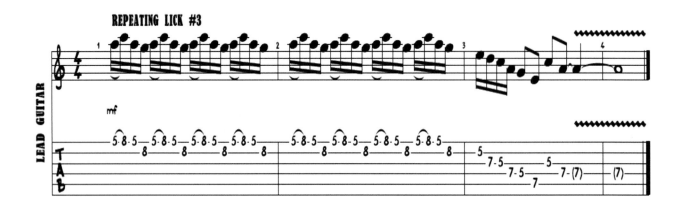

HISTORY OF ROCK

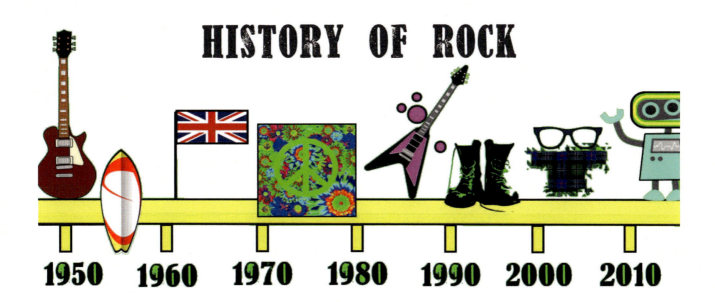

1950 1960 1970 1980 1990 2000 2010

BLUES

Since it's inception in the 1950s, rock music has been—and continues to be—influenced by the blues. For years, rock musicians used common blues techniques like call and response phrasing, the blues scale, and the 12-bar form. Created in the 19th century by African-Americans, famous blues guitarists include Robert Johnson, Muddy Waters, Jimmy Reed, Freddy King, B.B. King, Buddy Guy, & Albert King.

DECADE	GENRE	FAMOUS BANDS & ARTISTS	LEGENDARY GUITAR PLAYERS
1950S	ROCK 'N' ROLL ROCKABILLY	CHUCK BERRY BO DIDDLEY BUDDY HOLLY ELVIS PRESLEY	CHUCK BERRY BO DIDDLEY CHET ATKINS LES PAUL
1960S	BRITISH INVASION SURF ELECTRIC BLUES	THE BEATLES THE ROLLING STONES JIMI HENDRIX	GEORGE HARRISON JIMMI HENDRIX KEITH RICHARDS
1970S	GLAM ROCK PUNK ROCK SOUTHERN ROCK	DAVID BOWIE THE RAMONES ALLMAN BROTHERS LED ZEPPELIN	JIMMY PAGE ERIC CLAPTON DUANE ALLMAN
1980S	HEAVY METAL POP MUSIC INDIE	IRON MAIDEN QUEEN VAN HALEN METALLICA	EDDIE VAN HALEN BRIAN MAY PRINCE JAMES HETFIELD
1990S	GRUNGE ALTERNATIVE ROCK	NIRVANA GUNS N' ROSES PEARL JAM	SLASH TOMMY MORRELO ZAKK WYLDE
2000S	GARAGE ROCK EMO	THE STROKES THE WHITE STRIPES THE KILLERS MUSE	JACK WHITE JOHN MAYER MATTHEW BELLAMY
INSTRUMENTAL ROCK GUITAR OF ALL AGES	INSTRUMENTAL ROCK INCLUDES SURF, SHRED, BLUES, HARD ROCK, & METAL	THE VENTURES RACER X BOOKER T & THE M.G.S	YNGWIE MALMSTEEN, JOE SATRIANI, STEVE VAI, PAUL GILBERT, ERIC JOHNSON

BLACK BELT FOUNDATIONS TEST

I. 16TH NOTES

CLAP THE FOLLOWING RHYTHMS:

1.

2.

3.

4.

5.

II. REPEATING LICKS:

PLAY ALL THREE REPEATING LICKS OVER THE FOLLOWING CHORD PROGRESSION:

‖ A | G | A | G ‖

III. HISTORY OF ROCK

ARRANGE THE FOLLOWING DECADES WITH ITS CORRESPONDING ROCK GENRE:

A. INSTRUMENTAL ROCK MUSIC

B. 2000S

C. 1990S

D. 1980S

E. 1960S

F. THE BLUES

G. 1970S

H. 1950S

_____. BRITISH INVASION/ SURF/ ELECTRIC BLUES

HEAVY METAL/ POP MUSIC/ INDIE

_____. ALL DECADES

_____. ROCK 'N' ROLL/ ROCKABILLY

GLAM ROCK/ PUNK ROCK/ SOUTHERN ROCK

_____. GARAGE ROCK/ EMO

_____. GRUNGE/ ALTERNATIVE ROCK

_____. INCLUDES SURF, SHRED, BLUES, HARD ROCK, & METAL

LEARN, PLAY, & COMPOSE

☆	=	**BASS PART**
★ (yellow)	=	**CHORDS**
★ (green)	=	**MELODY**
★ (red)	=	**ALL PARTS + SOLO**
★ (black)	=	**ALL PARTS + SOLO + TEACH**

OPEN POWER CHORDS

E5

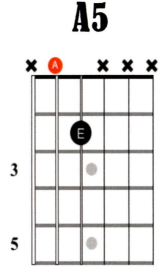

A5

D5

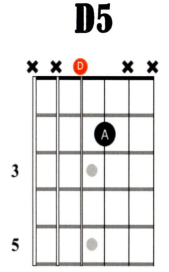

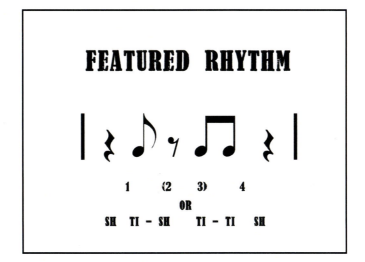

FEATURED RHYTHM

1   (2   3)   4
OR
SH   TI – SH   TI – TI   SH

LISTEN

- "WILD THING" – THE TROGGS
- "THE RUMBLE" – LINK WRAY
- "TNT" – ACDC
- "BREAKING THE LAW" – JUDAS PRIEST

PLAY

- POWER CHORD ROCK
- THUNDER ROCK

CHEAT SHEET: POWER CHORD ROCK

MUSIC BY BRIAN & SOPHIE PARHAM

CHEAT SHEET: THUNDER ROCK A-SECTION

MUSIC BY BRIAN & SOPHIE PARHAM

CHEAT SHEET: THUNDER ROCK B-SECTION

MUSIC BY BRIAN & SOPHIE PARHAM

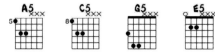

OPEN POWER CHORDS TEST

STEP 1: PLAY THROUGH THE FOLLOWING POWER CHORD PROGRESSIONS:

‖ E5　｜ D5　｜ A5 ｜ E5 ‖

&

‖ A5　｜ D5　｜ A5 ｜ E5 ‖

STEP 2: CORRECTLY NAME THE FOLLOWING OPEN POWER CHORDS:

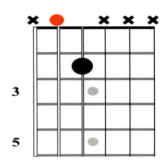 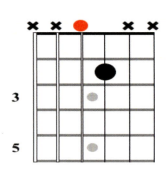 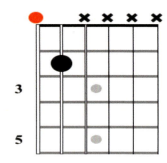

STEP 3: CLAP THE FOLLOWING RHYTHM:

STEP 4: PLAY ONE OF THE FOLLOWING TUNES:

- POWER CHORD ROCK
- THUNDER ROCK

OPEN POWER CHORDS:
COMPOSE A ROCK RIFF

STEP 1: CREATE A RHYTHM:

AVAILABLE RHYTHM CHOICES: 𝅝 𝅗𝅥 ♩ ♫ 𝄽

FOR EXAMPLE:

‖ ♫ ♩ ♩ ♫ ♩ ‖   ‖ 𝅗𝅥 ♫ ♫ ‖   ‖ ♩ 𝄽 𝄽 ♫ ‖

STEP 2: APPLY THE RHYTHM OF YOUR CHOICE TO A POWER CHORD PROGRESSION:

FOR EXAMPLE:

‖ E5 | D5 | A5 | E5 ‖

BONUS STEP: ROCK OUT!

COMPOSE YOUR OWN ROCK RIFF: OPEN POWER CHORDS

ROCK DOJO
GUITAR LESSONS FOR KIDS
Who Wanna Rock!

RHYTHM: _____

T
A
B

RHYTHM: _____

T
A
B

RHYTHM: _____

T
A
B

RHYTHM: _____

T
A
B

THE E NATURAL MINOR SCALE

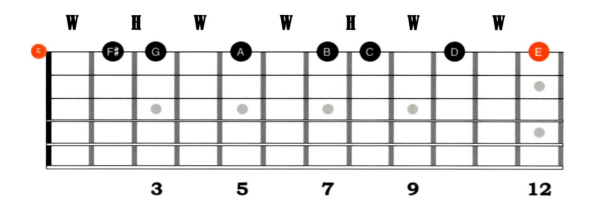

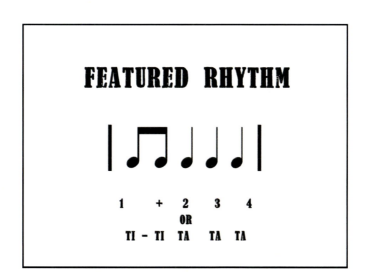

FEATURED RHYTHM

LISTEN

- "7 NATION ARMY" – THE WHITE STRIPES
- "WE WILL ROCK YOU" – QUEEN
- "PARANOID" – BLACK SABBATH
- "ELEANOR RIGBY" – THE BEATLES

PLAY

- SINGULARITY
- HEAVY RIFFIN'

CHEAT SHEET: SINGULARITY A-SECTION

MUSIC BY BRIAN & SOPHIE PARHAM

CHEAT SHEET: SINGULARITY B-SECTION

MUSIC BY BRIAN & SOPHIE PARHAM

59

CHEAT SHEET: HEAVY RIFFIN' A-SECTION

MUSIC BY BRIAN & SOPHIE PARHAM

CHEAT SHEET: HEAVY RIFFIN' B-SECTION

MUSIC BY BRIAN & SOPHIE PARHAM

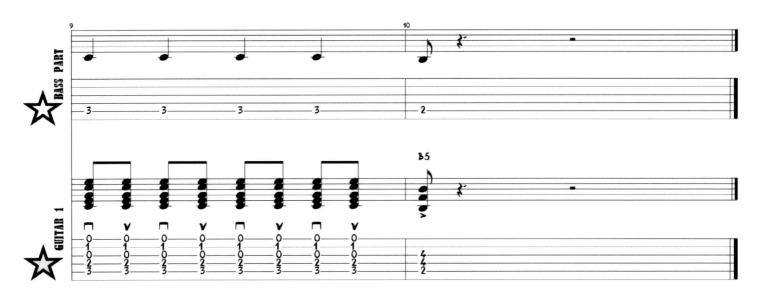

CHEAT SHEET:HEAVY RIFFIN' GUITAR SOLO

MUSIC BY BRIAN & SOPHIE PARHAM

THE E NATURAL MINOR SCALE TEST

STEP 1: THE E NATURAL MINOR SCALE IS BUILT USING THE FOLLOWING SET OF INTERVALS:

      A. WWHWWWH
      B. WHWWHWW
      C. W+HWWW+H
      D. WWHWWHW

STEP 2: COMPLETE THE E NATURAL MINOR SCALE ACROSS THE 6TH STRING:

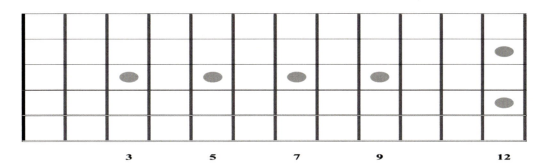

STEP 3: CLAP THE FOLLOWING RHYTHM:

STEP 4: PLAY ONE OF THE FOLLOWING TUNES:

- SINGULARITY
- HEAVY RIFFIN'

THE E NATURAL MINOR SCALE:
COMPOSE A ROCK RIFF

STEP 1: CHOOSE AN OPEN STRING (LOW E OR A):

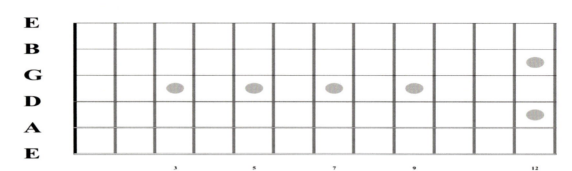

STEP 2: APPLY THE NATURAL MINOR SCALE TO THE STRING OF YOUR CHOICE (LOW E OR A):

EX. #1 THE NATURAL MINOR SCALE

IF YOU CHOOSE LOW E, USE ME: IF YOU CHOOSE A, USE ME:

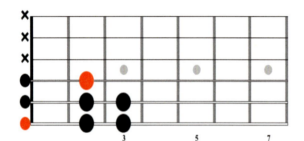   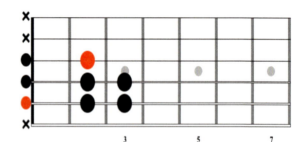

STEP 3: APPLY A PRE-SELECTED RHYTHMIC PATTERN:

EX. #2 PRE-SELECTED RHYTHMIC PATTERN (THIS IS AN EXAMPLE, YOU DO NOT HAVE TO USE IT FOR YOUR COMPOSITION!)

STEP 4: CREATE A SIMPLE TWO BAR PHRASE (QUESTION & ANSWER) USING THE PRE-SELECTED RHYTHMIC PATTERN:

EX. #3 THIS IS THE MAIN RIFF FROM HALLOWEEN THING. THIS SONG WAS COMPOSED BY A 12-YEAR-OLD ROCK DOJO STUDENT IN PORTLAND, OR.

STEP 5: FOLLOW THE ROCK RIFF FORMULA:

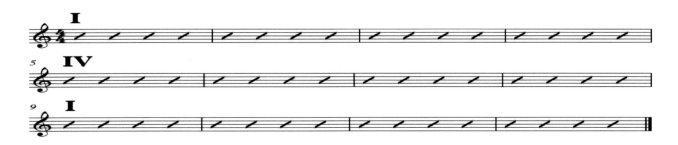

STEP 6: APPLY YOUR RIFF TO THE ROCK RIFF FORMULA:

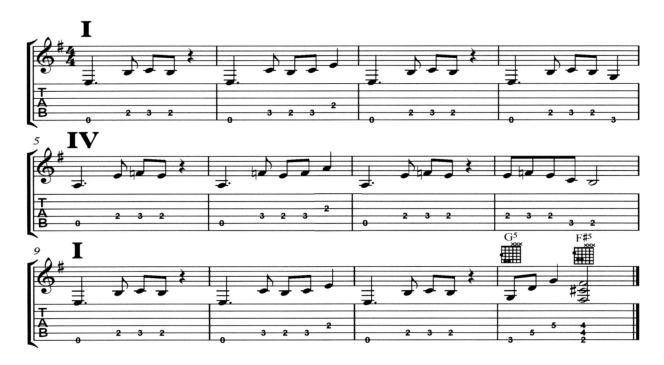

BONUS STEP: ROCK OUT!

COMPOSE YOUR OWN SONG:
E NATURAL MINOR

RHYTHM: _____

```
T
A    I        I        I        I
B
```

RHYTHM: _____

```
T
A   IV       IV       IV       IV
B
```

RHYTHM: _____

```
T
A    I        I        I        I
B
```

ROCK OUT!

SHIVER ME CIRCUITS, YE ROCK, MATEY!

THE F MAJOR PENTATONIC SCALE

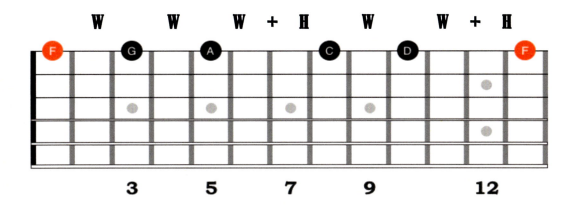

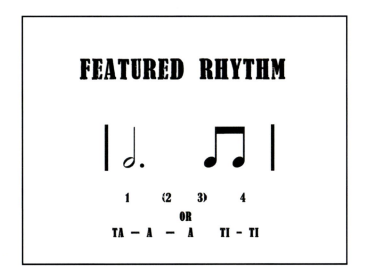

LISTEN

- "THE HOUSE OF THE RISING SUN" – THE ANIMALS
- "AMIE" – PURE PRAIRIE LEAGUE
- "SWEET HOME ALABAMA" – LYNYRD SKYNYRD
- "MY GIRL" – THE TEMPTATIONS

PLAY

- DAY BEFORE SUMMER
- SUNNY DAY

CHEAT SHEET:
DAY BEFORE SUMMER A-SECTION

MUSIC BY BRIAN & SOPHIE PARHAM

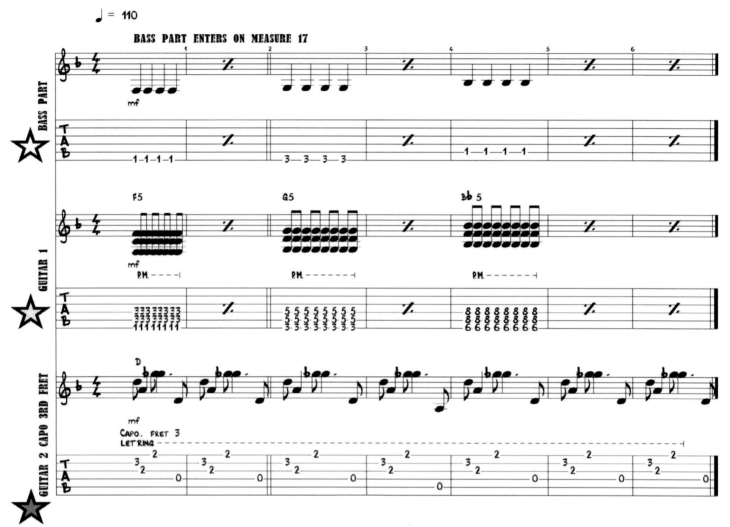

CHEAT SHEET:
DAY BEFORE SUMMER B-SECTION

MUSIC BY BRIAN & SOPHIE PARHAM

72

CHEAT SHEET: SUNNY DAY

MUSIC BY BRIAN & SOPHIE PARHAM

73

THE F MAJOR PENTATONIC SCALE
TEST

STEP 1: THE MAJOR PENTATONIC SCALE IS BUILT USING THE FOLLOWING SET OF INTERVALS:

A. WWW+HWW+H
B. WHWWHWW
C. W+HWWW+H
D. WWHWWWH

STEP 2: COMPLETE THE F MAJOR PENTATONIC SCALE ACROSS THE 6TH STRING:

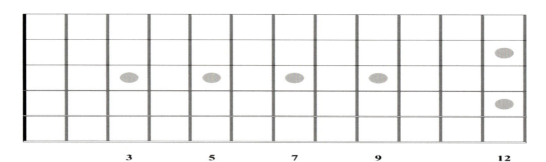

STEP 3: CLAP THE FOLLOWING RHYTHM:

STEP 4: PLAY ONE OF THE FOLLOWING TUNES:

- DAY BEFORE SUMMER
- SUNNY DAY

THE F MAJOR PENTATONIC SCALE:
COMPOSE A MELODY

STEP 1: VISUALIZE THE F MAJOR PENTATONIC SCALE:

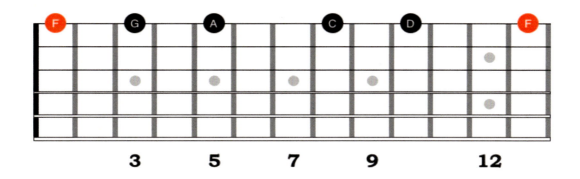

STEP 2: APPLY A PRE-SELECTED RHYTHMIC PATTERN:

EX: ‖♫ ♩ ♩ ♫ ♩‖ OR ‖♩ ♫ ♫ ♩‖ OR | ♩. ♫ |

STEP 3: CREATE A SIMPLE FOUR BAR PHRASE (QUESTION, ANSWER, QUESTION & DIFFERENT ANSWER) USING THE PRE-SELECTED RHYTHMIC PATTERN:

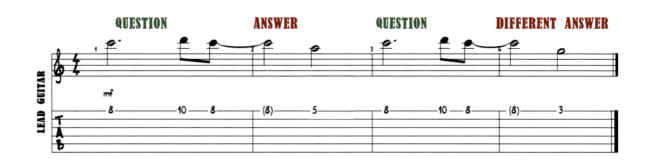

STEP 4: APPLY YOUR MELODY TO THE FOLLOWING CHORD PROGRESSION:

‖ F | DM | B♭5 | C5 ‖

COMPOSE YOUR OWN MELODY:
F MAJOR PENTATONIC

RHYTHM: _____

```
T |    F        DM       Bb5       C5
A |
B |
```

RHYTHM: _____

```
T |    F        DM       Bb5       C5
A |
B |
```

RHYTHM: _____

```
T |    F        DM       Bb5       C5
A |
B |
```

ROCK OUT!

YOUR SOUND SHAKES THE GATES OF VALHALLA!

THE E MINOR PENTATONIC SCALE

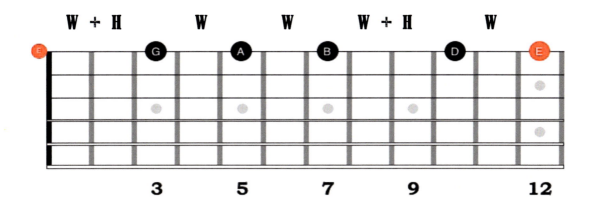

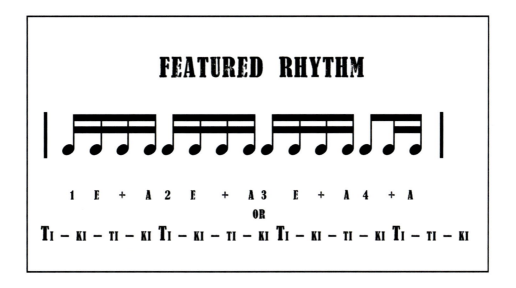

FEATURED RHYTHM

1 E + A 2 E + A 3 E + A 4 + A

OR

TI – KI – TI – KI TI – KI – TI – KI TI – KI – TI – KI TI – TI – KI

LISTEN

- "SUZIE Q" – CREEDENCE CLEARWATER REVIVAL
- "VOODOO CHILD (SLIGHT RETURN)" – JIMI HENDRIX
- "PRIDE AND JOY" – STEVIE RAY VAUGHAN
- "LONELY BOY" – THE BLACK KEYS

PLAY

- ICE BREAKER
- MINOR FIVES TO GO

CHEAT SHEET: ICEBREAKER A-SECTION

MUSIC BY BRIAN & SOPHIE PARHAM

MUSIC BY BRIAN & SOPHIE PARHAM

CHEAT SHEET: MINOR FIVES A-SECTION

MUSIC BY BRIAN PARHAM & J. STUART FESSANT

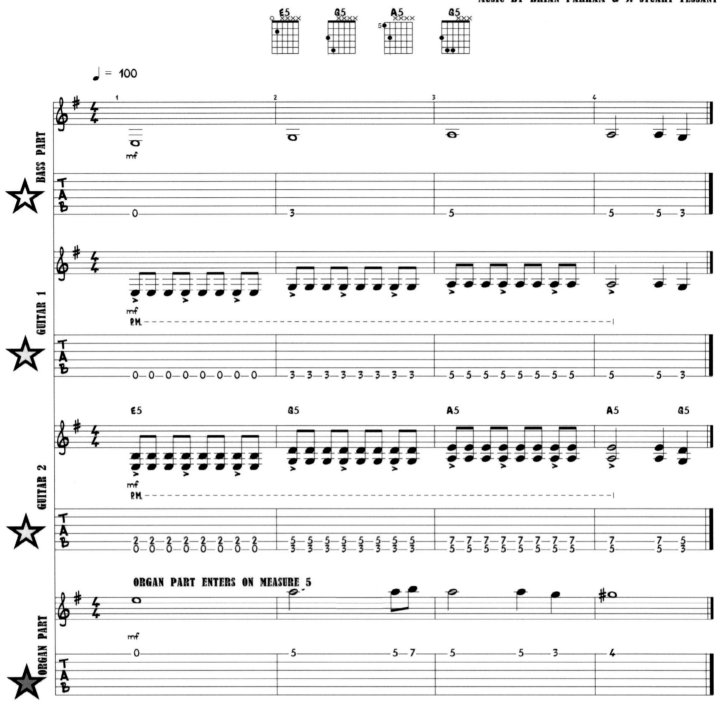

CHEAT SHEET: MINOR FIVES B-SECTION

MUSIC BY BRIAN PARHAM & J. STUART FESSANT

CHEAT SHEET: MINOR FIVES GUITAR SOLO

MUSIC BY BRIAN PARHAM & J. STUART FESSANT

♩ = 100

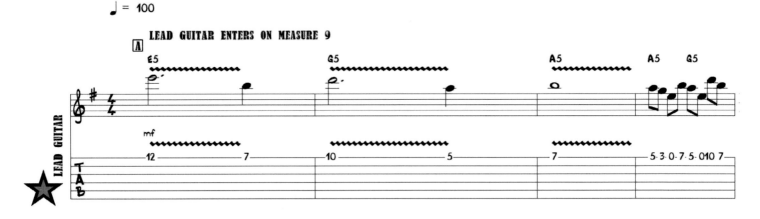

LEAD GUITAR ENTERS ON MEASURE 9

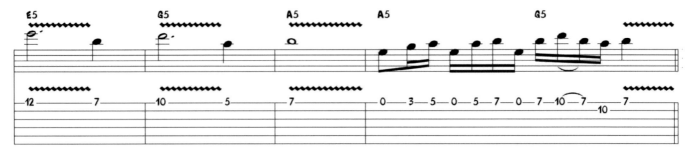

B-SECTION BEGINS ON MEASURE 17

THE E MINOR PENTATONIC SCALE
TEST

STEP 1: THE MINOR PENTATONIC SCALE IS BUILT USING THE FOLLOWING SET OF INTERVALS:

A. WWW+HWW+H

B. WHWWHWW

C. W+HWWW+H

D. WWHWWWH

STEP 2: COMPLETE THE E MINOR PENTATONIC SCALE ACROSS THE 6ᵀᴴ STRING:

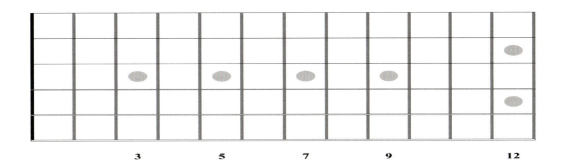

STEP 3: CLAP THE FOLLOWING RHYTHM:

STEP 4: PLAY ONE OF THE FOLLOWING TUNES:

- ICEBREAKER
- MINOR FIVES TO GO

THE E MINOR PENTATONIC SCALE:
COMPOSE A 12-BAR BLUES WITH THE MINOR PENTATONIC SCALE

STEP 1: APPLY THE MINOR PENTATONIC SCALE ACROSS THE 6TH STRING:

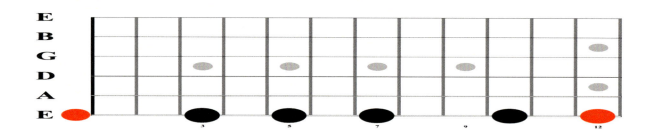

STEP 2: CREATE A SIMPLE TWO BAR PHRASE (QUESTION & ANSWER)

EX. #1 THIS RIFF WAS COMPOSED BY A URGD STUDENT AT BEVERLY CLEARY SCHOOL

QUESTION · ANSWER

STEP 3: APPLY THE BLUES FORMULA TO YOUR RIFF:

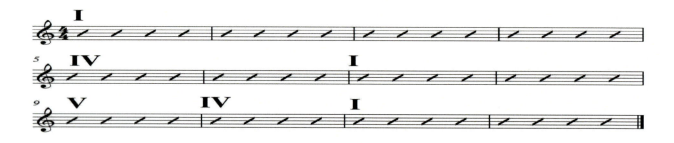

STEP 4: APPLY YOUR RIFF TO THE 12-BAR BLUES FORMULA:

EX. #2 THIS IS THE MAIN RIFF FROM ETHAN'S 12-BAR BLUES. THIS SONG WAS COMPOSED BY A 12-YEAR-OLD ROCK DOJO STUDENT IN PORTLAND, OR.

BONUS STEP: ROCK OUT!

COMPOSE YOUR OWN SONG: 12-BAR BLUES

RHYTHM: _____

```
T
A        I          I          I          I
B
```

RHYTHM: _____

```
T
A       IV         IV          I          I
B
```

RHYTHM: _____

```
T
A        V         IV          I          I
B
```

ROCK OUT!

I AM A PACIFIC RIM CHILD!

MOVEABLE POWER CHORDS

ROOT 6 POWER CHORDS

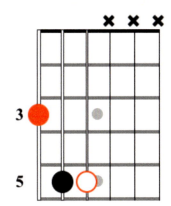

ROOT 5 POWER CHORDS

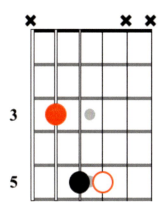

LISTEN

- "HIT ME WITH YOUR BEST SHOT" – PAT BENATAR
- "YOU REALLY GOT ME" – THE KINKS
- "SMELLS LIKE TEEN SPIRIT" – NIRVANA
- "IRON MAN" – BLACK SABBATH

PLAY

- INTERSTELLAR OVERDRIVE
- HARD TO THINK

CHEAT SHEET: INTERSTELLAR OVERDRIVE

MUSIC BY BRIAN & SOPHIE PARHAM

CHEAT SHEET: HARD TO THINK A-SECTION

MUSIC BY BRIAN & SOPHIE PARHAM

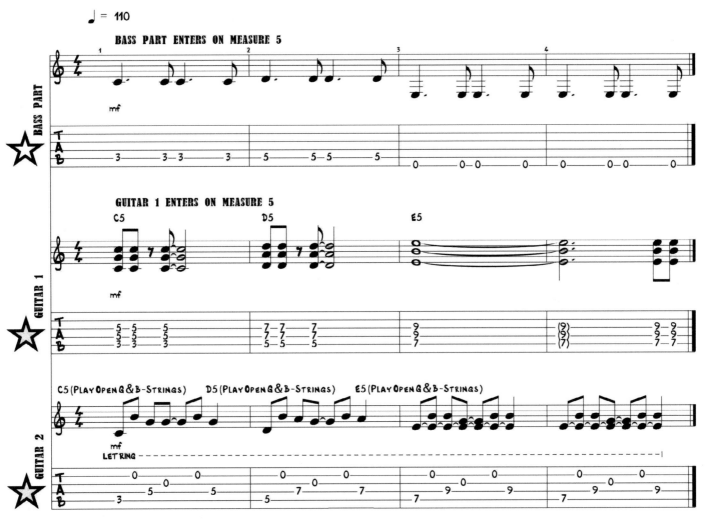

89

CHEAT SHEET: HARD TO THINK B-SECTION

MUSIC BY BRIAN & SOPHIE PARHAM

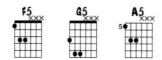

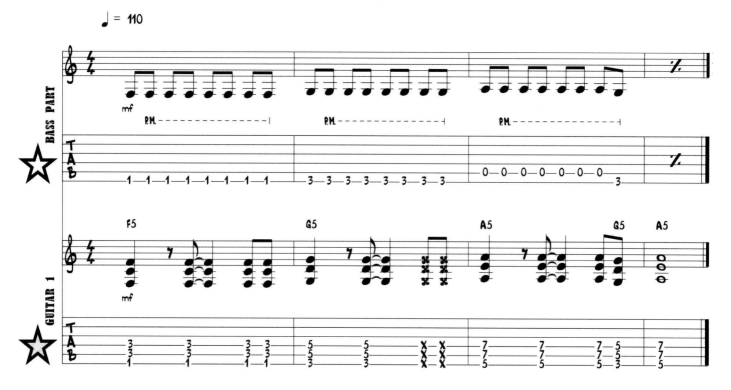

90

CHEAT SHEET:
HARD TO THINK GUITAR SOLO

MUSIC BY BRIAN & SOPHIE PARHAM

MOVEABLE POWER CHORDS TEST

STEP 1: LABEL THE NOTE NAMES ACROSS THE 6TH & 5TH STRINGS:

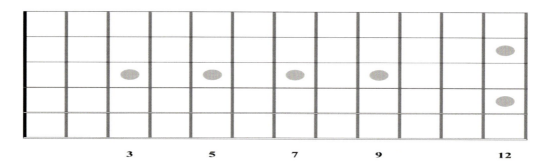

STEP 2: LABEL THE FOLLOWING MOVEABLE POWER CHORDS:

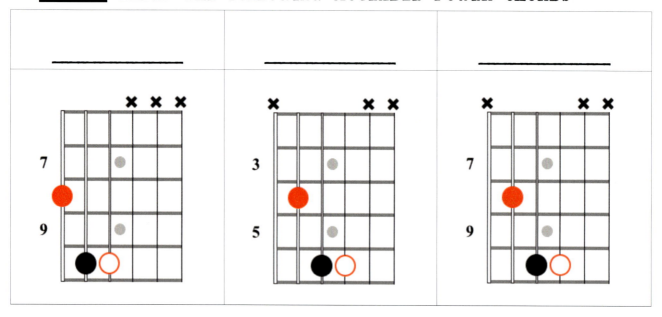

STEP 3: CLAP THE FOLLOWING RHYTHM:

STEP 3: PLAY ONE OF THE FOLLOWING TUNES:

- **INTERSTELLAR OVERDRIVE**
- **HARD TO THINK**

MOVEABLE POWER CHORDS:
COMPOSE A ROCK RIFF

STEP 1: CREATE A RHYTHM:

AVAILABLE RHYTHM CHOICES: 𝅝 𝅗𝅥 𝅘𝅥 𝅘𝅥𝅮𝅘𝅥𝅮 𝄽

FOR EXAMPLE:

EX: ‖ 𝅘𝅥𝅮𝅘𝅥𝅮 𝅘𝅥 𝅘𝅥𝅮𝅘𝅥𝅮 𝅘𝅥 ‖ OR ‖ 𝅗𝅥 𝅘𝅥𝅮𝅘𝅥𝅮 𝅘𝅥𝅮𝅘𝅥𝅮 ‖ OR ‖ 𝅘𝅥 𝄽 𝄽 𝅘𝅥𝅮𝅘𝅥𝅮 ‖

STEP 2: APPLY THE RHYTHM OF YOUR CHOICE TO A POWER CHORD PROGRESSION:

FOR EXAMPLE:

‖ B5 | G5 | A5 | B5 ‖

BONUS STEP: ROCK OUT!

COMPOSE YOUR OWN ROCK RIFF: MOVEABLE POWER CHORDS

RHYTHM: _____

```
T |--------|--------|--------|--------|
A |--------|--------|--------|--------|
B |--------|--------|--------|--------|
```

RHYTHM: _____

```
T |--------|--------|--------|--------|
A |--------|--------|--------|--------|
B |--------|--------|--------|--------|
```

RHYTHM: _____

```
T |--------|--------|--------|--------|
A |--------|--------|--------|--------|
B |--------|--------|--------|--------|
```

ROCK OUT!

WITHOUT POWER CHORDS, ROCK 'N' ROLL WOULD BE ROCK 'N' FLOP.

HALLOWEEN THING
A ROCK DOJO STUDENT COMPOSITION (NATURAL MINOR SCALE)
LUKE A. & BRIAN PARHAM

AMERICAN CLEAN - CHORUS

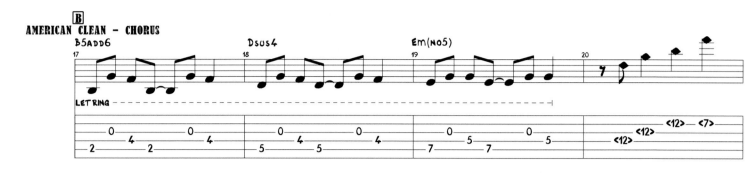

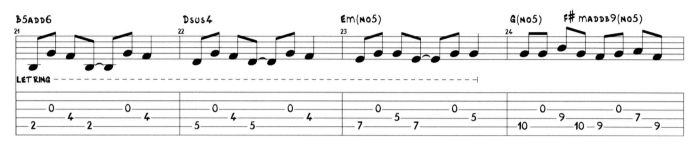

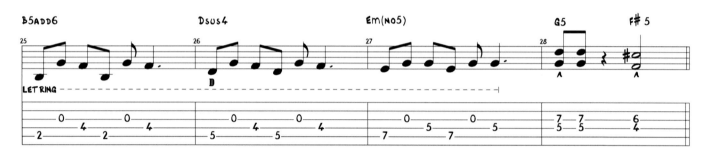

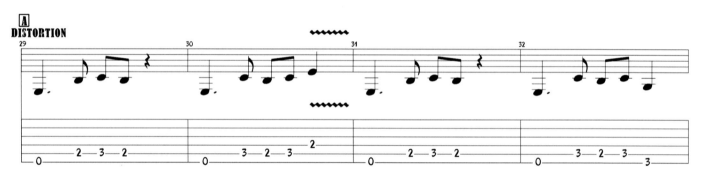

ZOMBIE BOY'S TOP 10 MUSIC JOKES

1	A MAN ASKS THE DEVIL: "HOW MUCH DOES IT COST TO BE THE GREATEST GUITAR PLAYER IN THE WORLD?" THE DEVIL SAYS: "GIVE ME YOUR SOUL." THE MAN ASKS: "WHAT CAN I GET FOR A DOLLAR?" DEVIL: "GREATEST BASS PLAYER IN THE WORLD."
2	Q. WHY ARE PIRATES GREAT SINGERS? A. THEY CAN HIT THE HIGH-C'S.
3	Q. HOW MANY GUITARISTS DOES IT TAKE TO CHANGE A LIGHTBULB? A. TWENTY. ONE TO CHANGE THE LIGHTBULB AND NINETEEN TO TELL EVERYONE HOW THEY COULD HAVE DONE IT BETTER!
4	Q. WHAT DO YOU CALL A GUITARISTS WHO KNOWS ONLY TWO CHORDS? A. A MUSIC CRITIC.
5	Q. WHAT DO YOU CALL A COW WHO PLAYS GUITAR? A. A MOO-SUCIAN
6	Q. WHAT'S THE MOST MUSICAL PART OF A TURKEY? A. THE DRUMSTICK!
7	Q. WHAT'S THE MOST MUSICAL PART OF A. A FISH? THE SCALES!
8	Q. WHAT'S THE MOST MUSICAL BONE? A. THE TROMBONE!
9	Q. WHAT'S A VAMPIRE'S FAVORITE PART OF THE GUITAR? A. THE NECK!
10	Q. WHAT MAKES MUSIC ON YOUR HEAD? A. A HEADBAND!

WWW.ROCKDOJO.ORG
(503) 484-641

MAZE TO GUITAR GREATNESS

START HERE

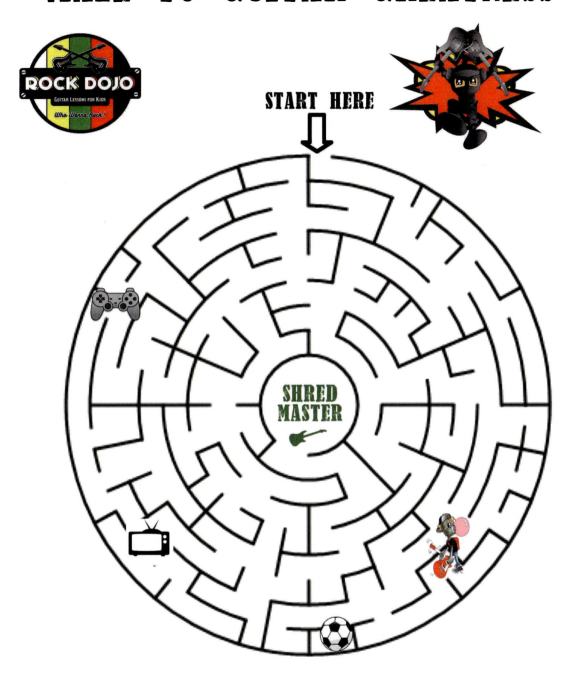

WORD SEARCH

WORD LIST

E B N H C J N T R W V G S B Y
N B L L I C K S E K W N U I M
R R A K J P J Y K M C F E P E
N T U S X H B N M K P T R O L
D Z P B S R H C F T X O G W O
M B O C B A P O I I S H R E D
R Y Y H B S J P E J L H T R Y
H J W E S I G A C A F M F C U
Y S S U S N B C O M Q H F H J
T M P O T G X T Q D H I Q O P
H L A F H U A I D Y R Z H R X
M E E U G P S O L O R U O D E
J L A A Y R F N R G P S M V W
M T C R D S I M P R O V I S E
W W E P O C K E T U Q V X M J

TEMPO
SHRED
SOLO
PHRASING
DRUMS
LEAD
IMPROVISE
BASS
JAM
LICKS
POCKET
RHYTHM
MELODY
POWERCHORD
SYNCOPACTION

WWW.ROCKDOJO.ORG
(503) 484-6417

CROSSWORD PUZZLE

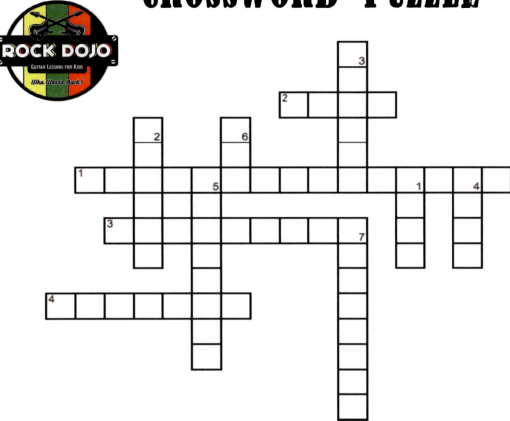

Across

1. These guitarists are responsible for laying down a steady groove while playing the chord progression of the song. A great _____ guitarist can take a simple set of chord changes (like C, G, D, & A) and voice them in a manner that adds interest, character, and expression to the overall sound.

2. A short musical statement. Just like words in spoken language, musicians combine these musical devices to tell compelling stories.

3. Two frets on the guitar.

4. Comes from a latin word which means to shake. Along with string bending, this technique adds a vocal like quality to lead guitar lines and are commonly used in rock, blues, and country music. This technique is performed by rapidly pushing and pulling the fretted strings.

Down

1. The short repeated musical phrases that keep you coming back again and again to your favorite songs.

2. The organized variation of note lengths in a piece of music.

3. The rhythmic glue that binds a band or a song together.

4. The section of the song featuring one of the musicians in particular, such as the keyboards, saxophonist, or the guitarist.

5. One fret on the guitar.

6. An informal musical event where musicians (usually instrumentalists) play improvised solos over tunes, vamps, or chord progressions.

7. When it comes to playing the guitar, it's not what you play, but how you play it. It's the use of rests, dynamics, and articulation—breathes life and emotion into music.

WHAT'S YOUR NINJA NAME & SIGNATURE MOVE?

THE MONTH YOU WERE BORN

1 = MIGHTY	4 = JUMPING	7 = TERRIFYING	10 = MIGHTY
2 = INVINCIBLE	5 = LIGHTNING	8 = DRAGON	11 = ROARING
3 = INDESTRUCTIBLE	6 = DREADED	9 = GLORIOUS	12 = IMPERIAL

+ YOUR FIRST NAME

A = KA	J = ZO	S = ARI
B = ZU	K = ME	T = CHI
C = MI	L = LA	U = DO
D = TE	M = RIN	V = RU
E = KU	N = TO	W = MEI
F = LU	O = MO	X = NA
G = JI	P = NO	Y = FU
H = RI	Q = KE	Z = ZI
I = KI	R = SHE	

+ YOUR AGE

0-5 = AIR GUITAR	8 = DYNAMICS OF DOOM	11 = KILLER VIBRATO
6 = POWER CHORDS	9 = BONE-CHILLING BENDS	12 = FEARSOME PHRASING
7 = TWO-HANDED TAPPING	10 = LETHAL LEADS	13 = SHREDDING

= _____

YOUR NINJA NAME & SIGNATURE MOVE

WWW.ROCKDOJO.ORG
(503) 484-6417

THE HATER

NAME: ZOMBIE BOY

ORIGIN: THE APOCALYPSE

FAVORITE BAND: MEGADEATH

FAVORITE SONG(S): "IT'S A WONDERFUL WORLD" BY THE RAMONES

THE MONSTER

NAME: TONY

ORIGIN: THE PACIFIC RIM

FAVORITE BAND: THE MONSTERS OF ROCK

FAVORITE SONG(S): 1. "GODZILLA" BY BLUE OYSTER CULT
2. "DIRTY PAWS" BY OF MONSTERS AND MEN

THE VIKING

NAME: BIG BJORN THE GUITAR BOLD

ORIGIN: NORSE GREENLAND DURING THE VIKING AGE BETWEEN THE 8TH AND 11TH CENTURY.

FAVORITE BAND: KING OF ASGARD

FAVORITE SONG(S): 1. "IMMIGRANT SONG" BY LED ZEPPELIN 2. "THE INVADERS" BY IRON MAIDEN

THE ROBOT PIRATE

NAME: CAPTAIN CORAL RIFF

ORIGIN: THE HIGH SEAS IN THE YEAR 3039 A.D.

FAVORITE BAND: IRON MAIDEN

FAVORITE SONG: 1. IRON MAN BY BLACK SABBATH
2. YOSHIMI BATTLES PINK ROBOTS BY THE FLAMING LIPS.

THE NINJA

THE NINJA IS SHROUDED IN SECRECY. HOWEVER, ONE THING IS CLEAR, SHE IS KILLER ON THE GUITAR.

YOU

THIS STORY IS YOURS TO WRITE:

NAME: _____

ORIGINS: _____

FAVORITE BAND: _____

FAVORITE SONG(S): _____

SAY WHAT? MUSICAL TERMS & DEFINITIONS

ABA FORM: A PIECE OF MUSIC WITH THREE SECTIONS. THE FIRST MUSICAL SECTION IS PLAYED (A), FOLLOWED BY A NEW SECTION (B), THEN BY A REPETITION OF THE FIRST SECTION (A).

AMP: GUITAR AMPS (OR AMPLIFIERS) ARE USED TO AMPLIFY THE WEAK ELECTRICAL SIGNAL FROM A PICKUP ON AN ELECTRIC GUITAR SO THAT IT CAN PRODUCE SOUND THROUGH ONE OR MORE LOUDSPEAKERS, TYPICALLY HOUSED IN THE AMP ITSELF.

ARTICULATION: THE WAY A NOTE IS PLAYED ON THE GUITAR. FOR EXAMPLE, GUITARISTS CAN SLIDE INTO NOTES, BEND UP TO NOTES, OR APPLY VIBRATO TO ADD CHARACTER AND PERSONALITY TO THEIR MUSIC.

CHEAT SHEET: A SIMPLIFIED MUSICAL SCORE DESIGNED EXCLUSIVELY BY THE ROCK DOJO TO HELP STUDENTS LEARN MULTIPLE GUITAR PARTS AS QUICKLY AND EASILY AS POSSIBLE. PLEASE NOTE: CHEAT SHEETS ARE NOT FULL MUSICAL SCORES.

CHORD: A CHORD IS A GROUP OF THREE OR MORE NOTES PLAYED TOGETHER AT THE SAME TIME. SOME GROUPS OF NOTES SOUND HAPPY (LIKE MAJOR CHORDS), SOME GROUPS OF NOTES SOUND SAD (LIKE MINOR CHORDS), AND SOME GROUPS OF NOTES SOUND AIRY AND AMBIGUOUS WHEN PLAYED TOGETHER (LIKE SUSPENDED CHORDS).

CHORD PROGRESSIONS: AS ATOMS ARE THE 'STUFF OF LIFE,' SO TOO ARE CHORD PROGRESSIONS THE BASIC BUILDING BLOCKS OF MUSIC. FROM BACH AND BEETHOVEN TO RIHANNA AND TAYLOR SWIFT, EVERY SONG YOU'VE EVER HEARD CAN BE REDUCED TO A SET OF REPEATING CHORD CHANGES KNOWN AS CHORD PROGRESSIONS.

DYNAMICS: THE SOFTNESS OR LOUDNESS OF A SOUND.

GROOVE: THE RHYTHMIC PROPULSION OF A BEAT OR A SONG. IF A BEAT HAS A GOOD FEEL TO IT, IT HAS GROOVE.

HARMONY: TWO OR MORE NOTES PLAYED AT THE SAME TIME. IN ANCIENT GREECE, HARMONY WAS USED TO DESCRIBE THE COMBINATION OF A LOWER NOTE WITH A HIGHER NOTE.

HALF STEP: A SINGLE FRET DISTANCE BETWEEN TWO NOTES ON THE GUITAR. FOR EXAMPLE, A HALF STEP ABOVE G (3RD FRET ON THE E-STRING) IS G# (4TH FRET ON THE E-STRING).

JAM: A JAM IS AN INFORMAL MUSICAL EVENT WHERE MUSICIANS (USUALLY INSTRUMENTALISTS) PLAY IMPROVISED SOLOS OVER TUNES, VAMPS, OR CHORD PROGRESSIONS.

IMPROVISATION: THE SPONTANEOUS CREATION OF MELODIES 'ON THE SPOT' OVER CHORD PROGRESSIONS.

LEAD GUITARIST: LEAD GUITARISTS PLAY MELODIES, PERFORM FILL-IN LICKS BETWEEN VOCAL LINES, AND SHRED HAIR-RAISING, SPINE-TINGLING, MIND-MELTING GUITAR SOLOS! IF YOU WANT TO BECOME A LEAD GUITARIST, YOU'LL NEED TO DEVELOP A SOLID COMMAND OF SCALES, LICKS, AND GUITAR TECHNIQUES LIKE BENDING AND VIBRATO. JUST TO NAME A FEW, ANGUS YOUNG, BRIAN MAY, AND SLASH ARE SOME OF THE FINEST ROCK LEAD GUITARISTS OF ALL-TIME.

LICK: A LICK IS A SHORT MUSICAL STATEMENT. JUST LIKE WORDS IN SPOKEN LANGUAGE, MUSICIANS COMBINE LICKS TO TELL COMPELLING STORIES.

MELODY: A MUSICALLY SATISFYING SEQUENCE OF NOTES. A GOOD MELODY IS SINGABLE, MEMORABLE, AND RECOGNIZABLE. MELODIES ARE OFTEN REFERRED TO AS 'TUNES.'

PHRASING: WHEN IT COMES TO PLAYING THE GUITAR, IT'S NOT WHAT YOU PLAY, BUT HOW YOU PLAY IT. THAT'S WHERE PHRASING COMES IN. PHRASING —OR THE USE OF RESTS, DYNAMICS, AND ARTICULATION—BREATHES LIFE AND EMOTION INTO MUSIC.

PLAYING IN THE POCKET: WHEN A MUSICIAN FINDS HIS/HER SPACE IN THE MUSIC WHILE SIMULTANEOUSLY LEAVING SPACE FOR THE OTHER BANDMATES TO OCCUPY.

POCKET: THE POCKET IS THE RHYTHMIC GLUE THAT BINDS A BAND OR A SONG TOGETHER.

RHYTHM: THE ORGANIZED VARIATION OF NOTE LENGTHS IN A PIECE OF MUSIC.

RHYTHM GUITARIST: RHYTHM GUITARISTS ARE RESPONSIBLE FOR LAYING DOWN A STEADY GROOVE WHILE PLAYING THE CHORD PROGRESSION OF THE SONG. A GREAT RHYTHM GUITARIST CAN TAKE A SIMPLE SET OF CHORD CHANGES (LIKE C, G, D, & A) AND VOICE THEM IN A MANNER THAT ADDS INTEREST, CHARACTER, AND EXPRESSION TO THE OVERALL SOUND. JUST TO NAME A FEW, STEVE CROPPER, BO DIDDLEY, AND THE EDGE ARE SOME OF THE FINEST RHYTHM GUITARISTS OF ALL-TIME.

RIFF: RIFFS ARE THE SHORT REPEATED MUSICAL PHRASES THAT KEEP YOU COMING BACK AGAIN AND AGAIN TO YOUR FAVORITE SONGS. FROM *KASHMIR* TO *THRIFT SHOP*, A GREAT RIFF CAN CAPTURE THE EAR AND CAPTIVATE THE IMAGINATION.

SECTION: A DISTINCT PART WITHIN A MUSICAL COMPOSITION.

SCALE: SCALE COMES FROM A LATIN WORD WHICH MEANS LADDER. PITCHES (OR NOTES) BEGIN AT THE LOWEST RUNG OF THE LADDER PROGRESSING STEP-BY-STEP FROM LOW TO HIGH. MUSICIANS USE SCALES TO COMPOSE MELODIES AND BUILD HARMONIES OR CHORD PROGRESSIONS.

SCORE: THE WRITTEN VERSION OF THE MUSIC INCLUDING ALL THE PARTS FOR EACH INSTRUMENT OF THE ENSEMBLE.

SHRED GUITAR: VIRTUOSIC LEAD GUITAR STYLE OF GUITAR BASED ON FAST

GUITAR PLAYING TECHNIQUES.

SOLO: A SOLO IS THE SECTION OF THE SONG FEATURING ONE OF THE MUSICIANS IN PARTICULAR, SUCH AS THE KEYBOARDS, SAXOPHONIST, OR THE GUITARIST. SOME MUSICIANS REHEARSE THEIR SOLOS—PLAYING THE SAME SOLO MORE-OR-LESS THE SAME WAY EVERY TIME—WHILE OTHER MUSICIANS IMPROVISE THEIR SOLOS. BELIEVE IT OR NOT, AN IMPROVISED SOLO IS MADE UP ON THE SPOT!

STRING BEND: A BASIC ELECTRIC GUITAR TECHNIQUE USED TO CHANGE THE PITCH OF A NOTE BY PUSHING UP OR PULLING DOWN ON THE STRINGS. STRING BENDS GIVE LEAD GUITAR LINES A VOCAL LIKE QUALITY AND ARE COMMONLY USED IN ROCK, BLUES, AND COUNTRY MUSIC.

STRUMMING PATTERN: A PRESET RHYTHMIC PATTERN FOR RHYTHM GUITARISTS.

SYNCOPATION: THE EMPHASIS OF WEAK BEATS IN MUSIC.

TEMPO: THE SPEED OF THE MUSIC.

THEME: A CATCHY & MELODIC SECTION OF A SONG.

VIBRATO: VIBRATO COMES FROM A LATIN WORD WHICH MEANS TO SHAKE. ALONG WITH STRING BENDING, VIBRATO ADDS A VOCAL LIKE QUALITY TO LEAD GUITAR LINES AND ARE COMMONLY USED IN ROCK, BLUES, AND COUNTRY MUSIC. VIBRATOS ARE PERFORMED BY RAPIDLY PUSHING AND PULLING THE FRETTED STRINGS.

VIRTUOSO: A PERSON WITH OUTSTANDING TECHNICAL MUSICAL ABILITY. JUST TO NAME A FEW, PAUL GILBERT, JOE SATRIANI, AND STEVE VAI ARE MODERN ROCK VIRTUOSOS.

WHOLE STEP: A TWO FRET DISTANCE BETWEEN TWO NOTES ON THE GUITAR. FOR EXAMPLE, A WHOLE STEP ABOVE G (3RD FRET ON THE E-STRING) IS A (5TH FRET ON THE E-STRING).

BELT TESTING

STUDENT'S NAME: _____

TEACHER'S NAME: _____

WHITE BELT ACHIEVEMENT

LEARN:

○ KNOW YOUR GUITAR: PARTS OF THE GUITAR, HOW TO TUNE YOUR GUITAR, NAMES OF THE OPEN STRINGS
○ PLAYING IN THE POCKET: BASIC RHYTHMS
○ THE MUSICAL ALPHABET

PLAY:

○○☆ GUITAR PART FOR 2 SONGS

COMPOSE:

○ YOUR OWN SONG USING THE FEATURED MUSICAL CONCEPT

GREEN BELT ACHIEVEMENT

LEARN:

○ OPEN CHORDS
○ AMP SETTINGS: DIAL IN THE PERFECT TONE
○ SYNCOPATED RHYTHMS

PLAY:

○○☆ GUITAR PART FOR 2 SONGS

COMPOSE:

○ YOUR OWN SONG USING THE FEATURED MUSICAL CONCEPT AND BASIC SONG FORM

YELLOW BELT ACHIEVEMENT

LEARN:

○ THE NAMES OF THE NOTES ON THE E & A STRINGS & MOVEABLE POWER CHORDS
○ GUITAR TABLATURE
○ ROCK BAND: THE ROLES OF EACH INSTRUMENT

PLAY:

○○☆ GUITAR PART FOR 2 SONGS

COMPOSE:

○ YOUR OWN SONG USING THE FEATURED MUSICAL CONCEPT

RED BELT ACHIEVMENT

LEARN:

○ ROCK SOLOING 101: THE PENTATONICS
○ THREE EASY LICKS
○ BASIC SONG FORM

PLAY:

○○☆☆☆ GUITAR PARTS FOR 2 SONGS
○ SOLO OVER SONGS

COMPOSE:

○ YOUR OWN SONG USING THE FEATURED MUSICAL CONCEPT

BLACK BELT ACHIEVEMENT

LEARN:

● ROCK SOLOING 102: REPEATING LICKS
● 16TH NOTES
● HISTORY OF ROCK GUITAR

PLAY:

●●★★★ GUITAR PARTS FOR 2 SONGS
● SOLO OVER SONGS

COMPOSE:

● CHOOSE TWO MUSICAL CONCEPTS AND COMPOSE A SONG WITH AN A & B SECTION

AND:

● HELP OTHER STUDENTS ALONG THEIR MUSICAL JOURNEYS!

ABOUT THE AUTHORS

BRIAN PARHAM

AS A KID, I HAD TWO DREAMS: ROCKIN' OUT ON THE GUITAR AND KICKIN' BUTT IN THE MARTIAL ARTS. UNFORTUNATELY FOR MY DREAMS, I GREW UP POOR IN RURAL PENNSYLVANIA. FATE, HOWEVER, INTERVENED PLACING A GUITAR IN MY HANDS AT THE TENDER AGE OF TWENTY-SIX, AND I HAVE NEVER LOOKED BACK!

APPROACHING THE GUITAR LIKE A MAD SCIENTIST, I IMMERSED MYSELF INTO A WORLD OF MUSIC PLAYING THROUGH EVERY METHOD BOOK I COULD CHECK OUT AT THE LOCAL LIBRARY, WATCHING EVERY INSTRUCTIONAL DVD I COULD GET MY HANDS ON, AND STUDYING WITH SOME OF THE FINEST TEACHERS ON THE PLANET INCLUDING LEGENDARY GUITARISTS PAUL GILBERT, MIMI FOX, AND JOHNNY NITRO.

I BECAME OBSESSED WITH DEVELOPING THE MOST EFFECTIVE AND ENGAGING SYSTEM FOR TEACHING KIDS TO PLAY ROCK GUITAR DURING THAT TIME. THE ROCK DOJO IS THE CULMINATION OF ALL MY STUDIES AND EXPERIMENTS IN MUSIC EDUCATION COMBINED WITH MY PASSION FOR THE GUITAR AND MY LOVE FOR THE MARTIAL ARTS.

OVER THE LAST FIVE YEARS, I WON NUMEROUS ACADEMIC AWARDS AND GRANTS FOR MY WORK WITH THE ROCK DOJO INCLUDING A 2017 REGIONAL ARTS AND CULTURAL COUNCIL PROJECT GRANT.

WITHOUT A DOUBT, MY LIFE WOULD NOT BE THE SAME WITHOUT THE GUITAR. LEARNING TO ROCK TAUGHT ME ABOUT THE POWER OF DISCIPLINE, GOAL SETTING, AND GRIT, EXACTLY THE SAME LIFE SKILLS I NEEDED TO BE SUCCESSFUL IN EVERY OTHER AREA OF MY LIFE.

TODAY, I LIVE IN PORTLAND, OR, WITH MY WIFE SOPHIE WHERE WE SHARE THE GIFT OF MUSIC. AS AN AMBASSADOR OF MUSIC, I AM DETERMINED TO BRING THE POWER OF ROCK MUSIC—AND THE TRANSFERABLE LIFE SKILLS LEARNING TO PLAY ROCK GUITAR INSTILLS—TO KIDS ALL OVER THE WORLD.

SOPHIE PARHAM

SOPHIE PARHAM IS THE CO-FOUNDER OF THE ROCK DOJO. SHE GREW UP IN FRANCE WHERE SHE BEGAN PLAYING VIOLIN AT AGE THREE AND STUDIED PIANO AND GUITAR LATER ON. SHE HAS BEEN TEACHING MUSIC IN NORTHEAST PORTLAND FOR THE PAST THREE YEARS, SERVING CHILDREN BETWEEN 6 TO 12 YEARS-OLD. SOPHIE IS PASSIONATE ABOUT PLAYING THE GUITAR, COMPOSING FOR CHILDREN, AND SHARING THE GIFT OF MUSIC IN HER COMMUNITY.

TO BE CONTINUED . . .

FOR MORE INFORMATION ABOUT THE ROCK DOJO, PLEASE VISIT
WWW.ROCKDOJO.ORG/
FOR INFORMATION ABOUT ILLUSTRATIONS, PLEASE EMAIL
DSMITH@GENERATIONCREATIVE.COM

Made in the USA
San Bernardino, CA
27 July 2017